Essays
on Strategy

Essays
on Strategy

*Selections from the
1983 Joint Chiefs of Staff Essay Competition*

1984

National Defense University Press
Fort Lesley J. McNair
Washington, DC 20319

CONTENTS

   Mr. David M. Ransom, Department of State
   Lieutenant Colonel Lawrence J. McDonald,
      US Marine Corps
   Mr. W. Nathaniel Howell, Department of State

   Mr. Kevin J. McGuire, Department of State
   Colonel Thomas D. Pilsch, US Air Force
   Captain John W. Stark, US Navy

FOREWORD

The essays you are about to read won recognition in the 1983 Joint Chiefs of Staff Essay Competition. Through this competition, the Joint Chiefs of Staff challenge students at our senior military colleges to propose new strategies for national security, encouraging original thought as opposed to traditional research and reporting. The 1983 competition included both individual and group essays, and both categories are represented in this book. The National Defense University conducted the judging and is pleased to publish this selection from the essays.

The five selected essays address issues and choices confronting Western strategists. "Operation Barbarossa" examines basic military strategy and delineates certain characteristics of the Soviet soldier by reviewing Germany's 1941 invasion of Russia. "Tantalus Revisited" traces efforts to ban the use of chemical weapons and analyzes current US and Soviet proposals for an international convention, paying particular attention to verification and compliance. The three remaining essays examine more specific strategic issues: how, or indeed whether, to implement "Deep Attack" concepts for defense of Central Europe; how the United States and its NATO Allies can develop a workable joint strategy for the Persian Gulf region; and how to improve the already good Australian-American relationship to increase security in the Indian Ocean region and Southwest Asia.

These essays emphasize the value of intelligent and open debate on national security issues.

Richard D. Lawrence
Lieutenant General, US Army
President, National Defense
University

1

OPERATION BARBAROSSA:
HITLER'S INVASION OF RUSSIA

by

Austin C. Wedemeyer
Colonel, US Air Force

Colonel Austin C. Wedemeyer, US Air Force, recently served as Deputy Commander for Operations, 5th Air Wing, Minot, North Dakota. He is currently assigned as Senior Air Force Adviser to the Naval War College in Newport, Rhode Island. Colonel Wedemeyer is a 1983 graduate of the Air War College.

BARBAROSSA—"MASTERPIECE OF CONQUEST"

No one starts a war—or rather, no one in his senses ought to do so—without first being clear in his mind what he intends to achieve by that war . . . .

Clausewitz

Barbarossa, the name given to the German invasion of Russia on 22 June 1941, was conceived as the "masterpiece of conquest." The plan was enormous in size and extremely optimistic in perspective. However, it was based on the proven effectiveness of the German Army and on German perceptions of weakened leadership and apparent ineffectiveness of the Soviet armed forces.

The plan looked like a page from Clausewitz—war as an extension of policy, well defined objectives, speed, and mass. But Hitler seems to have overlooked or purposely ignored many lessons of Clausewitz. Did Hitler take to heart the lessons contained in Clausewitz' critique of Napoleon's Russian campaign? Did he adequately consider chance and the friction of war? Barbarossa was designed to last only "6 to 10" weeks, but it lasted nearly 4 years and contributed significantly to the total defeat of the German nation.

WHY DID HITLER TURN TO THE EAST?

War is not a mere act of policy but a true political instrument, a continuation of political activity by other means.

Clausewitz

By August 1940, Hitler's armies had defeated and occupied the major states of continental Europe, except for the temporary but untrusted ally, Russia. The Germans had recently won stunning victories over Poland and France. At Dunkirk, a desperate evacuation had just saved 338,000 men from annihilation.[1] And the Battle of Britain, though as yet inconclusive, was underway. In this heady atmosphere, it seems, Hitler resolved to attack the Soviet Union.

Historians point to four factors that may have formed the basis for Hitler's decision. First, although temporarily weakened, Britain was a potential threat to Hitler's grandiose plans. Perhaps the biggest concern was that Britain might close ranks with Russia, entice the United States into the war, and thus attack Germany on two fronts. By defeating the Soviets in one quick campaign, Hitler could postpone or even completely eliminate the British threat.

Also, Russia's appetite for conquering new territories seemed almost as insatiable as Hitler's own. And a plan to divert the Soviets towards the south and east to carve up the British Empire did not interest Stalin.

In addition, the vast resources and *Lebensraum* of the Ukraine and the plains of European Russia attracted Hitler. The purges and mass executions of Soviet military leaders and the widespread dissatisfaction with the brutal, repressive Stalinist regime made this vast area ripe for the taking.

And finally, Hitler contended that National Socialism was philosophically incompatible with Communism, Bolshevism, and an "Eastern Europe filled with Jews." In Hitler's mind, "the Slavs were an inferior race and the Russians the most inferior of the Slavs."[2] He also identified "Jewish Bolsheviks" as "our deadly enemies."[3]

Having considered these four factors, Hitler satisfied himself that conflict with Stalin was inevitable. He then set about preparing for war with a vengeance.

4

THE STRATEGY OF BARBAROSSA

No conquest can be carried out too quickly and . . . to spread it over a longer period than the minimum needed to complete it makes it not less difficult but more.

Clausewitz

Hitler instructed his forces to prepare for the attack on the Soviet Union in Directive #21 of 18 December 1940:

The German Armed Forces must be prepared . . . to crush Soviet Russia in a rapid campaign ('Case Barbarossa'). . . . Preparations . . . will be concluded by 15th May 1941. . . .[4]

Some historians cite 15 May 1941 as the planned starting date for Barbarossa. The situation in the Balkans in early 1941, which caused Hitler to divert several armies to Yugoslavia and Greece, explains the 5-week delay before actual initiation. Others point to an unusually long winter and melting snow, which left the Russian roads soggy well into June 1941. However, historian Martin Van Creveld points to the "inability of German industry to supply the necessary material on time." [5] Many of the last units to be readied were supplied with captured French material.[6] 22 June was the date finally selected. In one of the classic ironies of history, Napoleon had chosen the same date for his invasion of Russia in 1812.

Hitler's plan envisaged that some "120–130 divisions" would defeat Russia by the end of the summer in a quick and decisive campaign. This emphasis on a rapid conclusion certainly followed the Clausewitzian approach to battle. Yet a note of caution is appropriate. Chance, as Clausewitz noted, is in the nature of war. And through the element of chance, "guesswork and luck come to play a great part in war." [7]

So confident were the Germans of a quick victory that many soldiers did not receive proper winter clothing. Some 14,000 German soldiers underwent major amputation operations due to frostbite during the winter of 1941–42.[8]

The general plan was to assemble overwhelming forces under a great cloak of secrecy and to strike with lightning speed into the Russian heartland, rolling over the surprised and unprepared Red Army along the way.

> The Russians were to be thrown off balance at the start and remorselessly pressed from that moment on; they were never to be permitted a breathing spell, a chance to gather their strength.[9]

In Directive #21, Hitler described the general intention of Barbarossa: "The bulk of the Russian Army stationed in Western Russia will be destroyed . . . Russian forces still capable of giving battle will be prevented from withdrawing into the depths of Russia." [10] This last assertion seems designed to avoid Napoleon's serious error of pursuing remnants of the Russian Army into the Russian steppes.

It was to be a gigantic, three-pronged attack along a 1,500-mile front, in which massive envelopments would crush the Red Army, leaving the way open to Leningrad, Moscow, and the Ukraine. The wide front would draw the enemy forward while spreading him thin. It would also tend to protect German lines of communication to the rear.

Hitler also used three other strategic principles of lesser, though still crucial, importance: mass, surprise, and speed. Although these are usually thought of as tactical concepts, Hitler developed and employed them on a scale that raised them to strategy. Their effective use at the beginning of Barbarossa gave them immense strategic value.

Mass. In his use of mass to create an overwhelming shock effect, Hitler built upon the guidance of Clausewitz: "Superiority varies in degree . . . it can obviously reach the point where it is overwhelming . . . . It thus follows that as many troops as possible should be brought into the engagement at the decisive point." [11] Clark saw Barbarossa as

> The head-on crash of the two greatest armies, the two most absolute systems, in the world. In terms of numbers of men, weight of ammunition, length of front, the desperate crescendo of the fighting, there will never be another day like 22nd June, 1941.[12]

Ziemke estimates total German strength committed to the start of Barbarossa at 3,050,000 men.[13] By way of comparison, Stokesburg calculates the total size of the Allied Expeditionary Force assembled in England for the Normandy invasion at 2,876,000; and Napoleon assembled "at least 450,000" in June 1812 for the invasion of Russia.[14] Barbarossa was total war on a grander scale than even Clausewitz was able to predict.

Surprise. The cloak of security surrounding Barbarossa was nearly absolute. Even Hitler's top field commanders were to be told at first that the plan was merely a "precaution." Hitler and Ribbentrop repeatedly denied, even to the German ambassador to the Kremlin, that there was any truth to the rumors of war floating around Moscow. British and American intelligence reports to the Kremlin gave ample warning of the attack. But Stalin passed them off as capitalist efforts to deceive him. Stalin, in fact, renewed efforts to meet agreed export levels of strategic materiel to Germany, at great sacrifice to the Soviets. The last trainload of strategic materials reached Germany in the hour that Hitler launched Barbarossa. Well after the start of the battle, German radio operators were still monitoring messages to Moscow such as, "We are being fired upon; what shall we do?" [15] Because of Stalin's obstinacy, the Soviets were totally unprepared for the attack.

Speed. If the Germans did not invent blitzkrieg warfare, they certainly brought it to perfection in Poland and France. No resource was spared to make Barbarossa the most spectacular example of lightning warfare. The progress of preparations and the intelligence reports of Soviet strength were so reassuring that, in February 1941, Hitler rendered the following judgment: "When Barbarossa commences, the world will hold its breath . . . . " [16] By the end of the first day, Manstein's 56th Corps had penetrated over 50 miles into Russian territory; resistance had not yet begun to stiffen.

Yet by 10 August, Army Group Center, having penetrated to a depth of 400 miles, discovered that they were behind Napoleon's 1812 timetable.[17] On 11 August, Chief of Staff Halder noted in his diary, "The whole situation makes it increasingly plain that we have underestimated the Russian Colossus." Perhaps the friction of war was beginning to make itself plainly felt. Clausewitz stated categorically that "the defensive form of warfare is intrinsically stronger than the offensive." [18] He seems to have predicted the course of the Russian campaign when he said,

> If defense is the stronger form of war, yet has a negative object, it follows that it should be used only so long as weakness compels, and be abandoned as soon as we are strong enough to pursue a positive object." [19]

ASSESSING THE STRATEGY

Bonaparte may have been wrong to engage in the Russian campaign at all; at least the outcome certainly shows that he miscalculated. . . .

Clausewitz

Hitler was a consummate politician. He well understood that war is an extension of policy. By precluding an alliance between Russia, Britain, and France, the German–Soviet Nonaggression Pact of 1939 allowed Hitler to carry out his aims in Poland and Western Europe. But once Europe was under Hitler's control, Stalin's turn would come. So when the instructions were given to prepare for an invasion of Russia, the German General Staff thoroughly and carefully planned for Operation Barbarossa. On paper, it was a textbook example of Clausewitz' approach to war. There was a well defined political objective—to crush Soviet Russia—and a clearly defined center of gravity to be destroyed—the Russian Army. Finally, there was the strategic application of mass, speed, and surprise.

Many would say that the political objective, conquest of Russia, was wrong in the first place. But Clausewitz would leave that determination to Hitler, just as he refused to pass judgment on Napoleon's decision to invade Russia: "We argue that if he was to aim at that objective, there was, broadly speaking, no other way of gaining it." [20]

Had history permitted Hitler and Clausewitz to discuss Barbarossa during the operation's planning phase, Clausewitz probably would not have opposed the invasion once Hitler's political decision was made. He had said of Napoleon more than a century earlier, "The risk of losing his army in the process had to be accepted; that was the stake in the game, the price of his vast hopes." [21] However, he probably would have counseled Hitler to read again about chance and friction in war.

Hitler clearly identified the destruction of the Red Army as a key objective. For Hitler, the Red Army was the Soviet "center of gravity." It represented not only the first obstacle in his path, but also the very life-blood and security base of the regime, the prop which held up the commissars and Stalin himself. No one would have understood more clearly than Hitler the direct link between the army and the dictatorial regime of

Stalin. Hitler and many of his officers felt that the Russian peasantry would rise up and throw off the regime even before the German Army had completely defeated the Soviets.

In more general terms, the whole of Russia west of the Urals was the objective. Hitler saw the vast potential of the resources and industrial capacity of Western Russia. However, Hitler and his generals disagreed somewhat, at least initially, about the importance of a direct drive on Moscow. If Hitler did not specifically identify Leningrad or Moscow as objectives, it was probably because he was certain all Russia would fall quickly before the *Wehrmacht*. Barbarossa was to be a geopolitical land-grab of historic proportions in the space of a summer. So even if Hitler had reread Clausewitz on chance in war, he probably would have considered the stakes high enough to take the gamble.

Hitler's mindset and perceptions are important in understanding his plan. He relied on the known capabilities of the Germany Army in blitz-krieg warfare and on the intelligence estimates of Soviet strength. He assumed that the Russian military leadership had been decimated in the purges of 1937-38 and that the Soviet soldiers would be baffled by a mechanized war. The Soviets were known to still rely on horse cavalry, of which there were some 34 divisions in 1937. Indeed, Clark shows photos of cavalrymen riding into battle with drawn sabres against Hitler's forces.[22] But horses sometimes have distinct advantages over tanks on Russia's muddy spring roads. And finally, Hitler's Achilles heel—illogical, irrational hatred and prejudice—colored his thinking and planning and limited his objectivity. The key to Hitler's downfall may very well have been his underestimation of the strength and patriotism of the Soviet citizen—the "will power and fatalism and that readiness to accept terrible sufferings that are essentially Russian qualities." [23]

Numerous parallels exist between the campaigns of Hitler and Napoleon. Clausewitz' assessment of Napoleon's 1812 campaign can be applied almost word for word to Hitler's 1941 Barbarossa:

> We maintain that the 1812 campaign failed because the Russian government kept its nerve and the people remained loyal and stead-fast . . . . The fault . . . lay in his being late in starting the campaign, in the lives he squandered by his tactics, his neglect of matters of supply and of his line of retreat.[24]

We might also point to the overconfidence, vanity, and hubris that these two men had in common. Neither seemed capable of owning up to a monumental error in judgment or of retreating, even when faced with certain disaster.

LESSONS FOR TODAY

It is legitimate to judge an event by its outcome, for this is its soundest criterion.

Clausewitz

In this analysis of Operation Barbarossa, two conclusions stand out. First, no matter how carefully an operation is planned, chance is always a factor. After calculating the probabilities of success, the wise planner will always build in a cushion and reserves to improve the opportunities for success. Military planners and strategists are always tempted to plan for a short, decisive war. This is probably a case of trying to reduce the uncertainties by emphasizing friendly strengths and enemy weaknesses in the short run. But it may also be an intuitive recognition that uncertainties multiply with time, and that the possibilities for the future course of events soon exceed the planners' ability to offer realistic solutions. The problems are magnified when whole nations commit themselves to a cause.

And second, one must never underestimate the Russian soldier's patriotism, his nationalism, or his love for "Mother Russia." Soldiers always seem to find additional inner strength when fighting for their homeland. This seems to be particularly true of the Russians. On the other hand, this trait leads to interesting speculation about how well ideology and nationalism would sustain the Soviet soldier in a long war outside his homeland. Recent Soviet performance in Afghanistan leaves that question open.

Ultimately, the analysis of Barbarossa supports Clausewitz' contention that war is filled with unknowns. Unknowns seem to be in particularly rich supply when war involves huge nations. More careful attention to the lessons of Clausewitz might have caused Hitler to reconsider his invasion of Russia. But this presupposes complete rationality, which we do not always attribute to Hitler.

For the Russians, living memories of World War II seem to have been a powerful deterrent to war. Let us hope that the deterrent does not die with the old soldiers.

Clausewitz would find much to recommend in the defensive orientation that the United States has chosen. Certainly he would support negotiations leading to arms reductions and political settlements. But we must glean our own lessons from Hitler's mistakes. They seem to be, do not attack the Russian on his home territory; if war comes, expect it to be long; and if war is long, plan on much uncertainty.

2

TANTALUS REVISITED:
THE BANNING OF CHEMICAL WEAPONS

by

F.M. Durel
Lieutenant Colonel, US Army

Lieutenant Colonel F.M. Durel, US Army, has been a chemistry instructor at the US Military Academy, where he was an Associate Professor, and at the US Naval Academy, where he was the Senior Army Representative. He is currently assigned as Chief, Nuclear, Chemical, and Biological Warfare Section, Supreme Headquarters, Allied Powers, Europe. Lieutenant Colonel Durel is a 1983 graduate of the Army War College.

THE US POSITION

The United States intends to eliminate "the threat of chemical warfare by achieving a complete and verifiable ban on chemical weapons."[1] Vice President of the United States George Bush stated this clearly before the United Nations Committee on Disarmament meeting in Geneva, Switzerland, on 4 February 1983. This seemingly simple and straightforward statement of US policy results from an evolutionary process in which the country has wrestled with divergent moral and pragmatic aspects of a deeply troubling issue.

Over many decades, the US position has vacillated between total acceptance and qualified rejection of chemical warfare (CW) as a means of waging war. Public interest has ebbed and flowed with a regularity determined to be coincident with the 11-year sunspot cycle.[2] No causal relationship has been established, but there can be no doubt that any elevation of CW matters in the public consciousness charges the air with emotional static electricity and disrupts established patterns of international discourse. This paper examines the controversial issue of chemical warfare and assesses the probability of US success in attempting to remove an old but infrequently used weapon from the arsenals of modern states.

Underlying the position expressed by the Vice President is a more complex and exact statement of US policy regarding CW. As expressed in the Fiscal Year 1983 Arms Control Impact Statements presented to Congress by the US Arms Control and Disarmament Agency (ACDA), current US policy is to

> improve defensive and deterrent retaliatory capabilities against the use of chemical weapons while working to achieve a complete and verifiable ban on their production, development, and stockpiling. As part of a credible and effective deterrent, the US seeks to achieve an adequate CW warning and protective capability and the ability and means to retaliate with chemical weapons in such a manner as to neutralize the advantages gained by enemy use of CW and to seek termination of the use of chemical weapons at the lowest level possible.[3]

15

Salient features of this policy statement can be grouped into two main points. First, the United States will seek to maintain an effective CW offensive capability as a deterrent, will employ chemical weapons only if used first against its own forces or its allies, and will maintain adequate defensive and protective capabilities. Second, it will accomplish these tasks while seeking a complete and verifiable ban on chemical weapons. In other words, in keeping with the positions taken in attempts to negotiate limitations on or reductions of nuclear weapons, the United States wants to bargain from a position of strength.

However, a serious asymmetry exists between US policy and the ability to implement that policy. Regarding the first aspect of the policy, in recent testimony before the Senate Armed Services Committee, General Bernard W. Rogers, the Supreme Allied Commander, Europe, stated,

> we do not have the proper types of chemical weapons that are necessary to deter their use by the Soviets. . . . The political guidelines under which I function say that I will be prepared to use chemical weapons in retaliation for the use against us by any aggressor. Under current conditions, I cannot fulfill that directive.[4]

This view is supported by the State Department, which indicated in a 1982 fact sheet, "our current chemical weapon stockpile . . . is inadequate to provide an effective deterrent."[5]

That such an asymmetry exists has been challenged, and one can find arguments to the effect that the US stockpile of chemical weapons is adequate to support US policy.[6] In addition, an analysis of the Fiscal Year 1982 Arms Control Impact Statements by the Congressional Research Service argues that a retaliatory capability becomes less important as improved protective measures reduce the vulnerability of forces to CW.[7] Regardless of the relative merits of the arguments, the United States is actively seeking to enhance its offensive CW capabilities by producing and stockpiling binary chemical weapons. Thus, the United States will align its chemical warfighting posture and its policy. If the United States is successful in these efforts to protect itself from an aggressor's use of chemical weapons and effectively retaliate in kind, how obtainable is the second aspect of the policy—the achievement of a complete and verifiable ban on chemical warfare?

PAST EFFORTS TO CONTROL CHEMICAL WARFARE

In the latter part of the nineteenth century, many attempts were made in the name of humanity to codify the customary rules by which nations waged war. One of the earliest attempts occurred in 1868 when the Russian czar convened an international military commission "to consider the desirability of forbidding the use of certain projectiles in time of war among civilized nations." [8] The "certain projectiles" the czar had in mind were those of a given size that were designed to explode upon impact, thereby causing more severe wounds and increasing the likelihood of death. In the minds of some legalists, this consideration of projectiles charged with "fulminating or inflammable substances" [9] is the first direct reference to chemical weapons and the first attempt to outlaw their use in warfare.

Regardless of the legalists' interpretation of the Declaration of St. Petersburg (as the deliberations of the czar's commission came to be known), the notion of projectiles charged with chemical substances began to receive increased attention. In 1899, the Hague Gas Declaration provided that the signatories "agree to abstain from use of projectiles the sole object of which is the diffusion of asphyxiating or deleterious gases." [10] In 1907, a follow-on conference specifically forbade the employment of poison or poisoned weapons.[11]

The events following the ratification of the Hague Gas Declaration by most of the European powers provide an interesting commentary on the fine art of international relations and arms control. The language of the declaration is highly restrictive, referring to the use of *projectiles*, the *sole* object of which is to emit gases. Germany, a signatory to the declaration, avoided violation of the treaty in World War I by using ground emplacement of chlorine cylinders (not projectiles) and releasing the gas into the prevailing winds. In addition, any number of projectiles can be designed to release gases in conjunction with another effect, such as blast or illumination. This quick analysis of the wording of the declaration points to a significant aspect of arms limitation agreements: the more general the wording, the less impact it will have; the more restrictive the wording, the easier it will be to circumvent.

As an interesting historical note, the United States, through its representative to the conference, Captain Alfred Thayer Mahan, did not accede to the declaration. Because no shells that emitted gases had yet been developed, Mahan had no evidence that such projectiles would be more or less humane than existing weapons. [12]

In 1922 the United States agreed to the provisions of the Washington Disarmament Conference. This agreement bound the signatory nations to a prohibition of use of "asphyxiating, poisonous or other gases, and all analogous liquids, materials or devices" in wars between themselves.[13] In principle, the United States sided with those nations seeking an abolition of chemical warfare. Apparently, the experiences of World War I caused US leadership to reconsider the position taken earlier by Mahan and actively seek to prohibit the use of chemical munitions. Note that the emphasis was still on prohibiting the use of chemical weapons, not on preventing the development, production, and stockpiling of such weapons.

After World War I, the various peace treaties signed by the allies and the defeated nations expanded the area of concern. These treaties forbade the manufacture and importation of CW agents, but only in regard to the activities of the defeated nations. No universal prohibition was attempted then, and no such intent found its way into subsequent efforts to outlaw chemical warfare.

Even in the famous Geneva Protocol of 1925, the emphasis was on preventing the use of chemical weapons in warfare and not on preventing their development, production, or stockpiling. In fact, many signatories to the protocol, the United States included, ratified or acceded with reservations—reservations that, for the most part, allowed retaliation in kind if prohibited weapons were used against them. In effect, the Geneva Protocol became a "no first use" policy for the signatory nations. As such, it recognized the necessity for these nations to maintain stocks of chemical weapons.

At the time, it appeared that the wording of the Geneva Protocol was acceptable to the United States. (In fact, the US delegation to Geneva had tabled the language of the prohibition in the first place.) But an intense lobbying effort by the Chemical Warfare Service, veterans groups, the American Chemical Society, and the National Association for Chemical Defense persuaded the Senate to refer the issue to the Foreign Relations Committee in December 1926. It remained dormant there, however, until 1947, when it was formally withdrawn in the full Senate.[14] General Douglas MacArthur reflected the US attitude toward chemical warfare during this period. Sterling Seagraves states that MacArthur's "attitude toward the thorny problems of chemical warfare was that a policy of prohibition was fine as long as nothing interfered with the ability of the United States to prepare for what was prohibited." [15]

The ink had hardly dried on the Geneva Protocol when many

countries began to believe the instrument was insufficient. They wanted measures to assure that no nations were preparing to conduct chemical warfare.[16] From then until now, under the auspices of both the League of Nations and the United Nations, various commissions, committees, and conferences have wrestled with ways to totally eliminate chemical weapons. In general, most delegations

> agreed that the weapons in question belonged to a category of arms most offensive and most threatening to civilians and therefore subject to qualitative disarmament, meaning that their possession or use should be absolutely prohibited. But absolute prohibition was deemed possible only if manufacture and storage of toxic substances and appliances for their employment, as well as training in their use, were also forbidden.[17]

The thorny issue was, and remains, how to assure that all parties are observing the details of a treaty that bans the development, production, and stockpiling of chemical weapons.

CURRENT EFFORTS

The 40-member Committee on Disarmament (CD) is currently meeting in Geneva, seeking an agreement between nations on the status of CW. The CD is an autonomous body linked to the United Nations (UN) through its secretary, who is the personal representative of the UN Secretary General. The 40 members of the committee include the five nuclear-weapon states (the United States, the USSR, the United Kingdom, the People's Republic of China, and France) and 35 other states that represent a wide range of interests but constitute a rough political and geographical balance.[18] The committee operates on a consensus basis, and through an ad hoc working group specializing in chemical warfare, it is seeking

> to elaborate a convention on the complete and effective prohibition of the development, production and stockpiling of chemical weapons and on their destruction, taking into account all existing proposals and future initiatives, with the view of enabling the committee to achieve agreement at the earliest date.[19]

Included on the agenda for committee action is the formulation of "effective verification methods in relation to appropriate disarmament measures, acceptable to all parties concerned." [20]

Since the breakdown of US–USSR bilateral negotiations in 1979, the CD has made some progress in formulating an acceptable agreement. But significant issues have yet to be resolved, especially in the areas of verification and compliance. The ad hoc working group has established nine open-ended contact groups; each is charged with investigating and debating a specific element of a chemical weapons convention. The nine elements of the convention being considered are as follows: Scope; Definitions; Declarations; Destruction, Diversion, Dismantling, and Conversion; General Provisions on Verification; Preamble and Final Clauses; National Implementation Measures; National Technical Means of Verification; and Consultation and Cooperation—Consultative Committee. The elements suggest the broad scope and complexity of the task before the ad hoc working group. They also dramatically illustrate the increased sophistication of international negotiations as compared to the early, inadequate attempts at limiting the use of chemical warfare.

The latest report of the CD, submitted to the thirty-seventh session of the UN General Assembly, provides the results of the working group's deliberations. A careful reading of the report does not give the reader an optimistic view of the near term attainability of a CW weapons ban. The contact group report on the General Provisions on Verification element was particularly vague and lacking in substance. This suggests that there are severe problems in that area. According to the 1981 Arms Control and Disarmament Agency annual report,

> constructive work was also accomplished in the areas of verification, and we and our allies were successful in obtaining broad support for adequate and effective verification of any CW prohibition. The difficulties and divergencies of view on specific verification measures, however, were illuminated more sharply than in the previous year.[21]

A translation of the "bureaucratese" of this report indicates there is not much to be encouraged about in the verification area.

VERIFICATION—THE BIG PROBLEM

In its simplest form, verification is intended "to provide assurance of compliance with the provisions of the convention." [22] In a more complex form, it is a process, specifically established or approved, by a disarmament agreement, carried out by individual state parties to the agreement, either reciprocally or not, or by an international body established or empowered to carry out the process, by personnel or technical means, in order to determine the degree to which the parties to the agreement have implemented its provisions and thereby observed or discharged their obligations under the treaty.[23]

In whatever form, the "basic function of verification is to gather information." [24] A broad view of the function of verification incorporates the following elements:

1. Deterrence of violation, inducing or enforcing compliance by the threat of discovery of violations.

2. Reassurance for the security of states through confirmation that a treaty is being implemented, or through a high probability of detecting violations if they occur; thus the function of confidence building.

3. Channel of communication.

4. Precedent for subsequent, more advanced stages of disarmament.

5. Mechanism for distinguishing between major and minor violations.[25]

In seeking a complete and verifiable ban of chemical weapons, the United States is emphasizing the second element mentioned above. The United States and the USSR—two superpowers, each possessing significant CW capabilities—have traditionally faced each other under a cloud of mistrust and doubt about the other's intentions. No statement by one goes unchallenged or unrepudiated by the other. Consequently, it seems only reasonable and proper that the United States should seek reassurance that its security is not being threatened by its adherence to a treaty.

The United States simply does not trust the USSR and does not want to be caught unaware if the Soviets violate any agreement. Note that a 1972 ban on biological and toxic weapons did not include any verification provisions, and the Soviets, a signatory to the convention, have since used toxic weapons in Laos, Kampuchea, and Afghanistan.[26] In the face of such blatant disregard for an international convention, critics of US arms control efforts are charging that it is pointless to sign any agreements with the Soviets. In recent Senate testimony, Lawrence Eagleburger, Under Secretary of State for Political Affairs, answered those critics. He said, "It is not that arms control is pointless: it is that we have to do a better job of it . . . if arms control is to work, agreements of this level must be fully and effectively verified." [27]

But the USSR is also proposing that provisions for verification be included in a convention. Therefore, it would seem that agreement should not be too difficult to achieve. Nothing could be further from the truth. In July 1982, the USSR tabled a proposal outlining the basic provisions of a convention. This convention would prohibit the development, production, and stockpiling of chemical weapons and require destruction or conversion of existing stockpiles.

Under the convention, verification of compliance would be based on a combination of national and international measures. The national measures would consist of the establishment of a Committee of National Verification, whose "composition, functions and methods of work should be determined by the State Party to the Convention in accordance with its constitutional forms." [28] This, in simple terms, is self-monitoring. The international measures mentioned in the proposal are also tantamount to self-monitoring. They require that verification be carried out through "consultations and cooperation between States Parties as well as through the services of the Consultative Committee of States Parties to the Convention." [29] This Consultative Committee would be made up of all parties to the convention and would have certain, as yet unspecified, responsibilities with respect to verification. In any event, if one state party has reason to suspect a violation on the part of another state party, and bilateral confrontation has been unsatisfactory, the matter could be placed before the Consultative Committee.

The USSR proposal provides that any state party receiving a request for information from the Consultative Committee "may treat this request favorably or decide otherwise." [30] Throughout the document, the USSR reveals itself as loath to allow independent, third-party verification. The only concession it makes to the need for international on-site inspections is a reference to a "possibility" in the areas of stockpile destruction and permitted production activities. [31]

In contrast to the USSR proposal, the US proposal submitted in February 1983 calls for recurring international on-site inspections of all areas covered by the convention, for the duration of the convention. The proposal even calls for the installation of sensors at declared CW facilities to permit the Consultative Committee to monitor activities. Each party would be "obligated to cooperate fully with the Consultative Committee in the exercise of its verification responsibilities." [32] These responsibilities would include conducting both systematic and ad hoc on-site inspections. Systematic inspections would be preplanned and agreed upon; ad hoc inspections would be those requested by a party and agreed to by at least five members of a fact-finding panel appointed by the Consultative Committee.[33]

The verification system proposed by the United States has been called "unprecedentedly complex and intrusive," but necessary to the realization of a suitable convention.[34] But the US position may not be as rigid as it seems at first glance. Ambassador Louis Fields, speaking before the Committee on Disarmament in February 1983, said, "we are not seeking absolute verification. We recognize that some risks will have to be accepted. However, we do insist that these risks will be minimized." [35] Whether this is just a statement of the obvious—nothing can be absolutely verified and risk will always be present—or a statement of the willingness of the United States to accept some middle ground with a higher level of risk is difficult to discern. But the US proposal is a good point of departure for negotiating because it represents the other end of the spectrum from the USSR proposal. Considerable room exists between the extremes for maneuvering and reaching a compromise position. The verification and compliance issue just may not be as intractable as it appears.

The difficulties associated with establishing an effective verification system vary greatly, depending primarily on the degree of technical sophistication of a country's chemical industry. The most severe challenge to a verification system occurs in highly industrialized countries capable of producing a broad range of CW agents. In general, CW agents can be classified into the following three groups: (1) those agents for which there is no legitimate peaceful use, (2) those normally produced in large quantities for industrial purposes, and (3) those agents which, as such, have no peaceful use but employ processes or intermediates which do.[36] An effective verification system will have to discriminate between these groups and provide a means for determining ultimate use. This is a difficult task, but not an impossible one.

Any country with a CW capability has to engage in one or more of the following activities: research, development, test and evaluation (RDTE); production; transport and storage; and training. These activities are subject to various types of search methods that can be used for verification purposes. The following table indicates these search methods and the activities against which they can be used most effectively.

Search Methods

Activities	Budgetary inspection [a]	Literature surveillance	Remote observation [b]	Economic analysis [a]	Inspection teams
Research	X				
Development	X	X [c]			X
Field testing and evaluation	X		X		X
Production of agents and weapons	X		X	X	X
Transport and storage	X		X		X
Training	X		X		X

Notes: [a] Applicable only in a country where there is open and unrestricted access to data.

[b] Sometimes referred to as national technical means.

[c] Open publication and discussion are generally agreed to be essential to stimulating and achieving good science. Secrecy at this stage would be counterproductive.

Source: Adapted from the Stockholm International Peace Research Institute, "The Prevention of CBW," *The Problem of Chemical and Biological Warfare,* 5:144.

Analysis of the table reveals that the most promising search method across the full spectrum of CW activities and applicable to all countries is the use of inspection teams. Use of inspection teams is also, without a doubt, the most intrusive method. A 1972 study by Midwest Research Institute (MRI) examined the reliability of inspections made on site and those made off site (at the plant perimeter). MRI concluded that plant perimeter inspections are of limited value unless there can be continuous observation.[37] The net result, then, is that effective verification requires on-site inspection, and the intrusion that goes with it is a necessary price to be paid for the security provided.

Techniques have been developed that can reduce the reliance on on-site inspection teams. Verification need not be 100 percent effective in order to fulfill its purpose.[38] Consequently, less effective methods than on-site inspections can be used, *provided they are used in conjunction with other, independent methods.* Simple probability theory shows that use of several independent, low probability verification methods increases the probability of detecting a violation.[39] Therefore, rather than relying on a single highly intrusive verification method, a treaty should be able to rely on several less intrusive methods, especially if intrusiveness is an overriding issue.

Matthew Meselson and Julian Perry Robinson have put forth another interesting argument for reducing the verification requirements of a treaty. In a 1980 *Scientific American* article, they wrote,

> It is important to note in this regard [that a verification system need only provide a high likelihood of detecting CW preparations on a scale large enough to constitute a major military threat] that the effectiveness of verification measures is enhanced by a high level of chemical defense. Good defense greatly raises the scale of chemical warfare preparation needed to constitute a major military threat, making concealment more difficult and intrusive inspection less necessary.[40]

Taking another approach, the Stockholm International Peace Research Institute (SIPRI) offers a rather startling argument concerning the lack of need for verification in a CW treaty where the parties possess nuclear weapons. The proposition goes as follows: Chemical weapons, given the current levels of nuclear weapons, make little impact on the overall balance of military strength; hence, an increased CW capability will not make a significant difference, and it is irrelevant whether the increase is detected or not. It is only when chemical weapons make a significant contribution to a nation's overall military strength that verification issues become important.[41]

Whether this argument is reasonable when nuclear parity and a significant disparity in chemical capability exist is open to question. For the narrow goal of achieving a chemical arms control treaty, it makes sense. However, if unreported violations (because no verification system exists) were to allow one party to gain or maintain a chemical capability and use it, the other party might have no recourse but to retaliate with nuclear weapons. Nuclear war would be a large price to pay for having achieved an unverified CW weapons ban agreement. Of course, this is the situation in which the United States and NATO find themselves relative to the USSR and the Warsaw Pact; and this is a prime reason the United States is attempting to improve its CW offensive capability through the development of binary munitions. The United States simply does not want to be drawn into nuclear conflict because of the use of chemical weapons.

HOPE FOR THE FUTURE?

In classical mythology, Tantalus was doomed to forever have the objects of his desires—fruit and drink—recede from his reach. In reviewing the past and current attempts to achieve an effective ban on the use of chemical weapons in warfare, it seems as if such a ban also will remain out of reach. The two prime players, the United States and the USSR, continue to tantalize one another with apparent concessions: the United States indicates that absolute verification is not necessary and the USSR offers a "possibility" of scheduled on-site inspections. Within the international forum of the Committee on Disarmament,

> the prevailing pattern, familiar from other arms control contexts, [is] that of a conversation being conducted at different levels simultaneously with little benefit to actual communication: from the East a broad-brush treatment stressing the supposed simplicity of the whole issue, from the West a preference for detailed analysis which emphasized its complexity, from most of the nonaligned a generalized impatience, and from the Swedish delegation a steady stream of working papers at a level of sophistication peculiar to Sweden.[42]

Given such an environment, is it reasonable to expect an agreement that meets the stated US goal of a "complete and verifiable ban on chemical weapons"?

To answer this question, one must consider the confidence building measures (CBMs) that have been built into the treaty proposals. The concept of CBMs originated in the negotiations of the Conference on Security and Cooperation in Europe (CSCE). Now the concept has spread to most other bilateral and multilateral deliberations on East–West issues, including the Committee on Disarmament. The fundamental purpose of CBMs is to generate trust between nations so that arms control and disarmament agreements can be achieved.[43] Within the framework of the current CW proposals submitted by the United States and the USSR, the CBMs are an integral part of the convention; they primarily involve declarations of current stockpiles, production plants, and agent filling facilities. This amounts to putting the cart before the horse, for a state party has to accede to the convention before the CBMs become operable. The CBMs need to be removed from the convention and kept as a series of preconvention agreements, leading up to a complete ban of chemical warfare.

Such a preagreement might be for the declaration of stockpile quality and quantity by a state party. Much has been written, both in open source and classified intelligence files, about the CW capabilities of nations; this information can serve as a basis for confidence building if it agrees substantially with a declaration. In the event of a mismatch, two possibilities exist—one where the declarations exceed intelligence information, the other where the opposite occurs. In the former case, the state party can assume faulty intelligence and can continue efforts to agree on a complete ban. In the latter case, the state party should recognize that the CBM has failed and that likelihood of achieving a ban is greatly decreased. The risks of signing an agreement without a satisfactory reconciliation of the differences would be too great and new initiatives would have to be derived and deliberated.

Some alternative CBMs could be exchange visits of technical experts to certain facilities. An example is the Pugwash Chemical Warfare Study Group's visit to the US chemical weapons disposal facility in Utah in 1979. Other alternatives could be exchanges of technical data or protective equipment, exchange visits between chemical warfare defense schools, or visits to munitions depots. Whether these and like measures were taken individually or collectively, their successful completion would generate a climate of increasing trust and build a foundation upon which a ban of chemical warfare could be achieved.

One concludes from the entire discussion that the US goal of a complete and verifiable ban of chemical weapons is not now attainable; the level of mistrust between the principal parties is too high. Any effort to reach agreement on a comprehensive convention will continue to fail until each state is confident that the treaty will not be violated by another state and that its own adherence to the provisions of the treaty will not jeopardize its security. Such confidence cannot be engendered by a single act. It must be nurtured and built over time through a series of successfully completed pretreaty agreements. A series of CBMs will steady the goal of banning chemical weapons and will allow that goal, unlike the elusive fruit and drink that Tantalus incessantly tries to reach, to be realized.

3

DEEP ATTACK IN DEFENSE OF CENTRAL EUROPE:
IMPLICATIONS FOR STRATEGY AND DOCTRINE

by

John R. Landry
Colonel, US Army

Malcolm B. Armstrong
Colonel, US Air Force

Howell M. Estes III
Colonel, US Air Force

Wesley K. Clark
Lieutenant Colonel, US Army

Boyd D. Sutton
Central Intelligence Agency

Colonel John R. Landry, US Army, has command and staff experience in Europe, including an assignment as Special Assistant to the Supreme Allied Commander, Europe. Colonel Malcolm B. Armstrong, US Air Force, has served primarily in Europe with forces committed to NATO. Colonel Howell M. Estes III, US Air Force, has extensive experience in Europe, including a tour at HQ US Air Forces Europe. Lieutenant Colonel Wesley K. Clark, US Army, has served in various locations, including Germany, and as Assistant Executive Officer to the Supreme Allied Commander, Europe. Boyd D. Sutton, Central Intelligence Agency, has specialized in Soviet and European military subjects for most of his career. All five authors are 1983 graduates of the National War College.

INTRODUCTION

In 1967, NATO's nations formally adopted the Flexible Response strategy and thus acceded to a long-held US view that deterring Soviet aggression requires strong conventional forces. Notwithstanding the bitterness and divisiveness of that decision, Alliance nations committed themselves to a series of ambitious defense programs to implement it. Execution of those programs has been neither uniform nor complete. But they have yielded a remarkable improvement in NATO's conventional forward defenses. In an absolute sense, Alliance forces are stronger today than at any time in their history.

But although Alliance forces have never been stronger, concern for NATO's ability to deter aggression has never been greater. The relentless pace of the Soviet buildup, both in terms of added force structure and improved armaments, outmatched Alliance defense efforts throughout the seventies. By the end of the decade, many analysts questioned whether existing defense programs were likely to produce a conventional defense equal to the needs of the Flexible Response. At the same time, few suggested that increased reliance on nuclear weapons made any sense, particularly in view of substantial Soviet strategic and theater nuclear force gains.

Even so, many Western defense analysts and government officials are optimistic that the Alliance can yet provide for a conventional defense sufficiently strong to make credible the Alliance's deterrent strategy. The source of this optimism is what are generally labeled Deep Attack concepts. These concepts reflect a renewed faith in the superiority of Western technology and the ability of NATO's forces to adapt technology to their tactical and strategic advantage. Emerging Deep Attack technologies—capabilities to locate, target, and destroy or delay enemy forces well forward of the line of contact—are believed to offer NATO an opportunity to offset quantitative superiority of Warsaw Treaty Organization (WTO) conventional forces.* Armed with such

---

*Integration of doctrine, technology, and force structure are discussed under "Doctrinal Implications of Deep Attack Concepts." The key weapon development programs and the timelines for their availability are discussed in appendix A; cost implications are treated in appendix B.

capabilities—some of which exist now—and employing appropriate doctrinal and procedural modifications, NATO's forces are thought to be capable of preventing the Soviets from breaking through Alliance forward defenses.

While generating optimism and intense interest in various technologies, Deep Attack concepts have also raised a number of issues. Many analysts, especially in Europe, question whether and how Deep Attack concepts will restore credibility to NATO's Flexible Response strategy. Some also question the wisdom of strengthening conventional capabilities; they see it as a move away from reliance on the nuclear deterrent that has provided for peace in Europe. In addition, whether potential Soviet responses to NATO's adoption of Deep Attack could enable the WTO to offset the new doctrine and weapons capabilities is not at all clear.

Deep Attack concepts have also raised doctrinal issues. The most fundamental question concerns the relationship between the objectives of Deep Attack and the scheme of ground maneuver. Another question concerns US and Allied views on allocation of airpower and procedures for air-ground coordination.

This essay addresses those issues by attempting to answer three questions. First, how can Deep Attack concepts be used to reinforce NATO's ability to deter aggression in Europe, or to improve NATO's chances for successfully implementing its strategy should deterrence fail? Second, how should US and NATO planners address the doctrinal and procedural issues that must be resolved if Deep Attack concepts are to be implemented? Finally, how will the Soviets respond to Deep Attack concepts, and how will their response affect the concepts' viability?

WHAT IS DEEP ATTACK?

Deep Attack concepts emerged from the interaction of three related but distinctly different influences: NATO concerns with the unrelenting buildup of WTO conventional forces in Central Europe since the late sixties; dissatisfaction with a defense doctrine widely regarded within the US Army as excessively reactive; and emergence of technologies that offer the potential for substantially better target acquisition and more lethal conventional weapons.

The outline of Soviet operational strategy in Central Europe has been clear for at least a decade. That strategy seeks a quick penetration of NATO's forward defenses and a rapid advance into the strategic depths of Alliance territory. The Soviet goal is to forestall full mobilization and reinforcement from the United States and to bring about early military and political collapse of NATO.

On the ground, the Soviets pursue this strategy by concentrating overwhelming force and by committing forces in succeeding echelons to maintain the momentum of combat operations. First echelon forces fix NATO's forward forces in position or destroy them. Second echelon forces complete the destruction of NATO's forward forces and flow through lines of least resistance to penetrate deeply into NATO's rear and disrupt the Alliance's ability to reinforce. WTO follow-on forces are thus critical to the overall strategy.

Meanwhile, WTO air forces hope to neutralize NATO's airpower. They will concentrate virtually the entire Western Theater of Military Operations' air capabilities against NATO airfields, ground based air defenses, nuclear storage sites, and command and control systems in a series of theater-wide strategic air operations. The WTO anticipates heavy losses but expects to cripple NATO airpower and to be able to deny NATO air superiority.

By the mid seventies, the WTO strategy and Soviet improvements in conventional doctrine, armaments, and force structure converged to create severe doubts about whether NATO could mount a credible direct defense. Two aspects of the Soviet buildup were particularly threatening. First, the Soviets appeared to be aiming for a short-warning attack capability by reducing their reliance on early reinforcement from the western military districts of the Soviet Union. Larger divisions armed with greater numbers of more advanced weapons, improved logistics support, and increased readiness were all part of this effort. These improvements threatened to reduce substantially both strategic and tactical warning. Thus, they would reduce NATO's ability to countermobilize, deploy forces forward, and prepare defensive positions.

Second, the Soviets launched an ambitious effort to achieve and maintain rapid attack advance rates. The Soviets concentrated on systems to exploit a high-speed attack. These systems included infantry combat vehicles, mechanized artillery, increased tactical aviation and helicopter gunships to provide continuous close support, and more effective antiaircraft weapons to suppress enemy airpower. Additionally, the Soviets emphasized development of more rapid and flexible command

and control procedures for ground, air, and air defense forces. Specific efforts focused on improving their capability to commit follow-on forces where and when they would achieve the greatest effect; to shift combat effort from one axis to another, depending on rapidly changing circumstances; and to coordinate the efforts of adjacent combat formations.[1]

Together, these trends attacked the credibility of NATO's Flexible Response strategy. They threatened to force an early political collapse of the Alliance before NATO could decide to escalate to the use of nuclear weapons. NATO must have a strong direct defense, capable of providing time for Alliance leaders to reach a nuclear decision, and confidence that continued resistance is militarily and politically feasible. Without such a direct defense, the very basis of Flexible Response is seriously eroded.

While US Army commanders in Europe were concerned with these trends, they were also disturbed by the Army's existing land force doctrine—the Active Defense. Many believed this doctrine was inappropriate to the nature of the Soviet challenge. They indicted Active Defense on three counts. First, it was excessively reactive; it ceded the initiative to the attacker by discouraging maneuver of forces against enemy vulnerabilities. Second, it focused too much on massing firepower at the point of an attempted Soviet breakthrough, where the enemy's strength was concentrated. Lateral movement of friendly forces in the face of WTO massed formations presents problems, and combat force ratios in these areas continuously and overwhelmingly favored the attacker. Finally, the doctrine seemed to endorse an attrition oriented defense. Therefore, it seemed to risk early exhaustion of forward forces by subjecting them to continuous operations against fresh, fully structured enemy units fed into the forward battle from reinforcing echelons. In short, Army commanders doubted the success of a doctrine that confronted wave after wave of echeloned WTO forces with a linear, positional defense.

As Army commanders wrestled with this problem, technological developments converged to offer some promise of offsetting Soviet quantitative superiority. Developments in a number of areas—particularly in sensors, data processing, terminal guidance, and conventional munitions effects—offered a potential for more effective engagement of mobile targets at extended ranges.

As the potential of these technologies became more apparent, proposals for their strategic and tactical application proliferated. Some spoke of strategically isolating the forward battlefield by destroying the enemy's capability to reinforce; others envisioned attacking key WTO command and control capabilities to deny the aggressor an ability to employ his echeloned formations effectively. Virtually all proposals suggested that emerging capabilities would reduce—some even said eliminate—NATO's reliance on nuclear weapons, both by stiffening the forward defense and by making conventional arms nearly as lethal as low-yield nuclear weapons.[2]

By the late seventies, these factors converged to produce doctrinal change, which incorporated emerging Deep Attack technologies. Two doctrinal concepts emerged in short order: the US Army's AirLand Battle doctrine and SHAPE's Follow-on Force Attack (FOFA) concept. Both of these concepts incorporated attacks on WTO follow-on forces to meet the increasing challenge of Soviet conventional force improvements.

The key assumption behind all Deep Attack concepts is that NATO and WTO forces *in the first echelon* are relatively evenly matched; therefore, NATO can provide a credible forward defense at the conventional level *if* it can keep WTO reinforcing echelons out of the forward battle, or at least allow them into it when and where most advantageous to NATO. This essential equivalence in the first echelon exists because NATO's forward defense policy requires placement of virtually all its ground combat power forward in the "first echelon." And while the WTO has more units and weapons theater-wide, terrain limitations, the need to operate somewhat dispersed because of the potential for use of nuclear weapons, and the basic WTO doctrine of operating from deeply echeloned formations all but preclude the WTO from using its theater-wide advantage at the line of contact. Using the inherent advantages of defense, and so long as the WTO's large follow-on forces can be held out of the forward battle, NATO's chances for a succesful forward defense are improved.

We now turn to the specific proposals and the issues they raise.

AirLand Battle Doctrine

The US Army began reevaluating its tactical doctrine during the late seventies. By early 1983, the Army's Training and Doctrine Command, working closely with the US Air Force's Tactical Air Command, had developed and gained the two Service Chiefs' approval for a new doctrine called AirLand Battle.* AirLand Battle doctrine focuses on combat operations of the corps and subordinate elements. It seeks to win battles,

---

*AirLand Battle doctrine was published in a revised US Army Field Manual, FM 100–5, on 20 August 1982. By early 1983, the Chief of Staff, US Air Force, expressed his support for the new doctrine.

not wars, recognizing that successful military operations are indispensable but are insufficient to guarantee victory.[3] Finally, it seeks to employ existing weapons and forces more effectively rather than prescribing development of new ones.[4] Thus, while recognizing that it would benefit from technologies that should be fielded in the next several years, it does not depend on them.

Within the limits noted above, AirLand Battle doctrine attempts to deny success to an aggressor's attack by seizing and maintaining the initiative.[5] To do this, the doctrine specifies the need to break the momentum of the enemy's attack, to destroy synchronization among the elements of attacking forces, and to defeat those forces piecemeal. Two battles must be fought simultaneously and in close coordination: a forward battle against committed units; and a deep battle against uncommitted forces, both to delay and disrupt their commitment to the forward battle and to create opportunities for subsequent maneuver against them. While the doctrine seeks a balance between maneuver and firepower, it particularly emphasizes maneuver. Maneuver is the way to concentrate strength against enemy weaknesses and gain a position of operational advantage from which to mass effective fires against enemy vulnerabilities.[6]

At the outset, AirLand Battle recognizes that Deep Attack—or the deep battle, as it is termed—is a prerequisite to successful execution of the doctrine. Because the doctrine focuses on corps operations, it envisions the conduct of the deep battle out to 100–150 kilometers—the limit of the corps commander's area of influence. US Army Field Manual 100–5 specifies that the corps commander's area of influence extends far enough beyond the Forward Line of Own Troops (FLOT) to "engage enemy forces which can join or support the main battle within 72 hours." The geographical extension represented will vary according to the commander's mission, the enemy, the terrain, and friendly forces available. In general, the geographic limits of the corps commander's area of influence will not exceed 100–150 kilometers.

Deep Attack delays and disrupts the reinforcement of uncommitted enemy forces and limits their availability for commitment to a time and place in the defender's advantage. Thus, Deep Attack both creates the opportunities for maneuver and permits its execution. All capabilities under the control of or provided in support to the ground commander (such as artillery, air support, electronic warfare, and deception), as well as the maneuver of friendly ground forces, are available to execute the deep battle. Of these, the Army recognizes that "battlefield air interdiction"—a NATO term not yet accepted into US joint doctrine—is the primary means of fighting the deep battle at extended ranges.[7]

The SHAPE Follow-on Force Attack Concept

Shortly after assuming responsibilities as Supreme Allied Commander, Europe (SACEUR) in 1979, General Rogers tasked the SHAPE staff to develop a concept for holding Soviet follow-on forces at risk with deep conventional fire. The SHAPE concept seeks to locate and track WTO forces during their entire process of deployment—from garrison to battlefield commitment—and to attack them when and where they are most vulnerable. The concept aims to exploit particularly critical enemy vulnerabilities in the reinforcement process: the rigidity of planning for an echeloned offense, the density of forces along limited attack routes, and critical transportation facilities.

Like the AirLand Battle doctrine, SHAPE's Follow-on Force Attack concept seeks to link the deep battle with the combat operations of forces in contact. But the means of doing so are vastly different. The SHAPE concept, unlike AirLand Battle, does not seek to synchronize the deep battle with the ground commander's scheme of maneuver. Instead, the SHAPE concept focuses on the centralized application of all Deep Attack assets to separate first echelon and second echelon forces. Success in this task will maintain NATO-WTO combat force ratios in the first echelon at a manageable level.

Issues Surrounding Deep Attack

Deep Attack concepts have received enthusiastic support from many quarters in NATO. But two major issues have caused continuing, often heated debates: the ambiguity of the concepts' implications for strategy and the persistence of doctrinal disagreements regarding the relationship of Deep Attack to the forward battle, including the allocation and control of airpower. Moreover, questions have arisen regarding the accuracy of underlying assumptions about Soviet doctrine and measures the Soviets might take to counter AirLand Battle, the SHAPE concept, or Deep Attack in general.

The strategic issue in this debate derives from European suspicion about American planning. The Europeans fear that strategic nuclear parity has driven American planners toward either a conventional or a limited nuclear defense option to escape the risks of a strategic nuclear exchange inherent in NATO's Flexible Response strategy. Either option is abhorrent to Europeans. The first raises the specter of a conventional Central European conflict every bit as devastating for Europeans as a nuclear conflict. The second threatens to confine a nuclear conflict to Europe. Regardless of the outcome of such a conflict, NATO Europe would emerge a strategic loser due to the devastation. Today, as in the past, US strategic nuclear guarantees are viewed by West Europeans as indispensable to a workable deterrent strategy.

Understandably then, any defense initiative that even remotely suggests a modification of Flexible Response will draw immediate fire in NATO. Deep Attack concepts have been caught in this fire, not because they challenge Flexible Response but because they have not been recognized as prerequisite to it. In short, Deep Attack concepts must be securely linked to NATO's current strategy if they are to receive Alliance support.

Doctrinal issues are multiple. First, where on the battlefield should NATO focus the brunt of its Deep Attack capabilities? (This question addresses both existing capabilities and those to be developed in the future.) By its very nature, AirLand Battle generally favors attacking enemy follow-on echelons located within the corps commander's area of influence (that is, within 100–150 kilometers of the FLOT). Other doctrinal proposals seemingly favor attacking enemy forces at much greater depths. The SHAPE concept seems to favor neither, although staffs at both SHAPE and AFCENT appear to favor deeper interdiction. For now, however, they recognize that the range of most current Alliance air and missile systems precludes concentrating efforts in a deep interdiction battle. This issue affects both decisions on the evolution of air-ground procedures and, more importantly, the design of future area surveillance, target acquisition, and Deep Attack systems.

Second, where in the command structure should NATO integrate air and ground operations? AirLand Battle seeks integration at the corps level; the SHAPE concept favors integration at the army group and region levels. Current procedures for allocating air support to and coordinating air interdiction operations with the ground battle generally support the SHAPE concept; they are inadequate to support AirLand Battle.

Finally, Soviet strategy for conventional operations in Europe clearly requires a consistently high tempo of attack leading to early, decisive breakthrough of NATO's forward defense. Although Soviet doctrine leads to the echeloning of forces—from the battalions in contact to second echelon regiments, divisions, armies, and even *fronts* moving forward from the western USSR—the bulk of Soviet combat power is forward with the first echelon divisions; that is where they believe the decisive battle will be fought. Recent weapons developments and changes in force structure have already added to the combat power of forward forces. And the Central European terrain would allow the WTO to put even more divisions in the first echelon. These developments and a wide range of options available to the Soviets raise questions about the underlying assumptions and the durability of AirLand Battle and the SHAPE concept.

These strategic, doctrinal, and enemy force issues combine to pose severe obstacles to the implementation of Deep Attack concepts. We now turn to those issues.

DEEP ATTACK AND
NATO'S FLEXIBLE RESPONSE STRATEGY

Alliance deliberations regarding the political acceptability and military utility of Deep Attack concepts will turn first and foremost on their implications for NATO's strategy. To some extent, this is true because various US authorities have emphasized the concepts' strategic value. But more importantly, Europeans are concerned that new doctrinal designs indicate possible shifts in the agreed strategy of Flexible Response.

The reluctance of US and NATO officials to state publicly the strategic implications of SHAPE's Follow-on Force Attack concept and the Army's AirLand Battle doctrine has contributed to this unease.* In the absence of such a statement, misconceptions have dominated the debate, often in ways that cause many allies to suspect the worst. Consequently, European suspicions threaten to derail valuable adjustments to NATO's tactical doctrines—adjustments that could make NATO's Flexible Response strategy more credible—and to slow the exploitation of promising new conventional technologies.

We will now identify the sources of European concern; demonstrate how Deep Attack concepts can be consistent with and essential components of NATO's Flexible Response strategy; and recommend a way to

---

*This seems to be changing. For example, an article on the subject by General Rogers appeared in the February–March 1983 edition of *NATO's Sixteen Nations*.

strengthen Flexible Response through adaptation of various elements of Deep Attack concepts.

European Concerns

At the outset, we must recognize that influential segments of the European NATO community have supported Deep Attack concepts as potentially productive in strengthening the Alliance's conventional capabilities. For example, Sir Julian Critchley, the British Conservative Party's Defense Committee Vice Chairman, has given a strong endorsement. In an article written for the *Daily Telegraph* in November of 1982, Critchley supported both Senator Sam Nunn's call for NATO to adopt AirLand Battle concepts and General Rogers' outline of the need for a Deep Attack capability.[8] Similarly, Manfred Woerner, Defense Minister of the Federal Republic of Germany (FRG), has urged the exploitation of emerging technologies.[9] And General Meinhard Glanz, Inspector General of the Bundeswehr, has stated explicitly the need to prevent the reinforcement of Soviet follow-on forces to assure a strong forward defense.[10] Despite these endorsements, however, major concerns remain.

Europeans are primarily suspicious that the new doctrinal concepts will either provide the basis for a conventional deterrent capability independent of nuclear escalation or lay the foundation for warfighting in which the use of nuclear weapons is confined to the European theater. The French explicitly communicated concern over the first of those possibilities in response to a 30 September 1982 speech by SACEUR in Brussels. In that speech, General Rogers noted the significant advantages to be gained by exploiting technology to attack WTO follow-on forces. He also observed that NATO's technological edge permitted development of such a capability and commented that a 4 percent gross national product (GNP) allocation to defense by all NATO nations would suffice to procure it.[11] The French newspaper *Le Monde* charged that the concept was a move toward a "no early use" policy for nuclear weapons—believed to be no better than a "no first use" pledge. It also decried the apparent shift in American perceptions of the role of nuclear weapons to deterring destruction rather than invasion. *Le Monde* also questioned how firmly the United States would continue to support Intermediate Range Nuclear Force (INF) deployments if longer range nuclear systems became secondary to conventional Deep Attack capabilities.[12]

The French have been the most vocal and explicit in their critique of Deep Attack concepts. Indeed, they have been the most critical of any defense initiative that appears to erode the credibility of Alliance nuclear deterrence. But other European nations share the concerns from which those criticisms arise. Many Europeans, particularly the West Germans, share the French concern that the decoupling of US strategic nuclear guarantees from the defense of Europe is one of the greatest dangers facing the Alliance today. While most Europeans—not the French—recognize the need for improved conventional forces to make credible Flexible Response, many suspect the US intention in pushing hard for such improvements. They believe the US proposals are driven more by a desire to avoid a nuclear decision altogether than by a desire to make credible NATO's threat to escalate a conflict if necessary. Those who hold this view point to the "no first use" advocacy of former US officials as confirmation of their position.[13] Europeans fear this development because it would eliminate the incalculability of risks confronting the Soviet Union. Thus, it would lower the threshold of conventional aggression.

We should not be surprised, then, that Europeans are distressed when various Deep Attack advocates suggest that emerging conventional technologies "may provide a conventional military power so formidable as to rival in the tactical arena the deterrent effect nuclear weapons have had on strategic war." [14] Such views focus on what many Europeans believe is a dangerous conception—that a successful conventional option by itself is capable of deterring Soviet aggression.

On the other hand, some Europeans believe that the new US concepts of Deep Attack may call for both nuclear and conventional capability, and that this could lead to plans for the use of nuclear weapons in a warfighting role. They find such a strategy even more frightening than the drive for a conventional-only option. During the Enhanced Radiation Weapon debate in Europe, Manfred Woerner, then a leading West German CDU/CSU defense spokesman, made clear the rejection of a theater nuclear warfighting doctrine confined to Central Europe.

> It is equally clear that a separation of tactical nuclear weapons from the strategic nuclear level is absolutely unacceptable for us Europeans.
>
> The territory of the USSR cannot be allowed, in theory or practice, to become a sanctuary in the nuclear phase of a conflict in Europe. The Soviet Union cannot be invited to contemplate a war limited to Western Europe, or even to German territory. Moscow must at all times be forced to reckon with the full ladder of escalation.[15]

Some Europeans have noted with concern several briefings of Air-Land Battle. These briefings reportedly discussed nuclear targeting decisions that might imply the need for early, perhaps even preconditional, release authority for NATO commanders to use nuclear weapons.[16] And of course, since AirLand Battle doctrine remains focused at corps operations or below, discussions of nuclear use are generally confined to warfighting implications. This fact is understandable, but it has disturbing implications for Europeans nonetheless.

Some NATO nations, particularly West Germany, are also sensitive to assertions that AirLand Battle doctrine envisions the conduct of strategically offensive ground operations. The FRG has accepted Deep Attack concepts in general. But the Bundeswehr's Inspector General has been extremely careful to reject any notion that German forces are, or will be, structured logistically to attack deep into WTO territory.[17] In part, rejection of such capabilities reflects NATO's defensive orientation. But it also acknowledges that the specter of an offensively capable Bundeswehr is acceptable neither to the Soviets nor to the FRG's continental allies.

Finally, the European media have suggested occasionally that the maneuver oriented AirLand Battle doctrine constitutes a retreat from the Alliance's concept of a forward defense.

These concerns may be erroneous and inconsistent. But they reflect considerable confusion regarding strategic versus tactical purposes of Deep Attack concepts and the doctrinal context to which the concepts are related. This confusion highlights the need for a militarily sound and politically acceptable justification for Deep Attack concepts if we are to continue the considerable progress attained to date.

Strategic Rationale for Deep Attack

The litmus test for determining the political acceptability of Deep Attack concepts is to see how well they support and reinforce Flexible Response. For the Europeans, doctrinal conformance to the Alliance's agreed strategy is a measure of continued US commitment to the defense of Europe and US willingness to share the risks as well as the benefits of Alliance membership.

To be consistent with Flexible Response, Deep Attack concepts must be clearly portrayed and understood as part of a strong direct defense. As such, their purpose must be expressed as defeat of less than full-scale conventional attacks and deterrence of massive conventional aggression by making credible Alliance threats of deliberate escalation. This suggests that Deep Attack concepts must satisfy at least three conditions.

First, they must contribute to an effective forward defense of Alliance territory. Pact forces must be unable to force a political collapse of NATO, either by a limited attack or by seizure of significant territory early in a large-scale conflict. Deep Attack must contribute to a direct defense capable of providing time for Alliance authorities to reach and execute a nuclear decision. Reaching such a decision would be anguishing for all NATO nations; each will seek to assure that all alternatives short of escalation have been exhausted. Without time afforded by strong conventional forces, such a decision probably could not be reached, and the credibility of Flexible Response would be correspondingly eroded.

Second, conventional Deep Attack must not conflict significantly with NATO execution systems or procedures for deliberate nuclear escalations. In addition, it must not alter perceptions concerning NATO's means and capabilities for nuclear escalation.

Third, insofar as Deep Attack vies with NATO's nuclear systems for its development resources or political commitment, Deep Attack concepts must be seen as inextricably integrated with NATO nuclear plans and systems. Deep Attack must not be viewed as an alternative to nuclear escalation, either in war plans or in forces developed for their execution.

As concepts for Deep Attack continue to unfold, clearly they can, but not necessarily will, meet these conditions. Surely all advocates intend that their concepts strengthen NATO's conventional direct defense. But the precise contribution of any Deep Attack concept to this purpose will depend not only on funding levels, but also on the situation and conditions extant at the outbreak of hostilities. Nor need the execution of Deep Attack in a period of hostilities conflict with NATO's means and capabilities for deliberate escalation. Separate attack systems can be developed, different control procedures can be employed, and different targets can be struck.

In this regard, however, we must note that efforts to portray second- and third-generation improved conventional munitions as having effects equivalent to those of low-yield nuclear weapons constitute a two-edged sword. These portrayals support, on the one hand, the feasibility of conventional Deep Attack. On the other hand, they suggest Deep Attack's availability as a substitute for nuclear weapons. Careful examination of the characteristics of these conventional weapons suggests that they are substitutable for only the very lowest-yield nuclear systems—the systems that, for reasons of collateral damage restraint, would tend to be employed relatively near friendly positions. By no means can such conventional systems substitute for the effect of the medium size nuclear weapons that might be contemplated for use against deeper enemy targets.

This consideration also suggests that, properly articulated and understood, conventional Deep Attack concepts cannot stand as an independent strategy for two reasons. First, the deterrent effects of the risks attending escalation to nuclear weaponry would be absent. Conventional weapons, no matter how destructive, do not convey a threat of escalation to strategic nuclear warfare. Therefore, they cannot substitute for the deterrent effect of tactical nuclear weapons. Second, the strictly military (warfighting) impact of improved conventional munitions could not foreseeably compensate for the absence of these risks. However, the improvements in reconnaissance and attack means attendant to Deep Attack have immediate application for more militarily significant deeper strikes with nuclear systems.

Strategic Pitfalls

Several pitfalls remain in developing and articulating the rationale of Deep Attack. First, we must properly describe the effect of a Deep Attack policy on the nuclear threshold. To suggest that Deep Attack will raise the nuclear threshold is to imply to some that the ultimate aim is a conventional defense. To focus on the other alternative—a lowered nuclear threshold—seems to suggest some sort of nuclear warfighting, which also raises concerns. The purpose of NATO's strategy is to deter aggression, not simply to prevent the conflict's escalation to the nuclear level. To the extent that improvements in NATO's defenses contribute to the former, they will most effectively assure the latter. Deep Attack must be viewed and addressed in precisely this perspective.

A second pitfall associated with emerging Deep Attack concepts is that they complicate the establishment of priorities. NATO's capacity to defend against a short-warning attack is eroding, and Alliance–WTO balances in the forward echelons of the battlefield are becoming more disparate. Even so, some Deep Attack advocates urge the Alliance to devote significant resources toward development of a technological capability to attack deep into WTO territory. If economic constraints did not exist, that capability, combined with greater capabilities in the first echelon, would be most welcome. But constraints do exist, and the Alliance must ask where it would most profitably apply marginal increments in resources.

Strategically, first priority must be accorded to the most dangerous threat to NATO. Currently, and for the foreseeable future, this is the capability of WTO forces to quickly break through NATO's forward defenses. As explained earlier, development of this capability has received priority in WTO defense improvements and is believed to be a prerequisite to Soviet operational strategy in Central Europe. So current and projected Alliance initiatives must aim toward denying such a capability.

The Alliance must direct its priority efforts toward blunting the attack of first and second tactical echelons of WTO forces and those operational follow-on echelons close to the forward battle. Interdiction of strategic follow-on echelons moving forward from the USSR must take a lower priority. The forward forces are already located in Eastern Europe during peacetime. They are the ones to be committed in the very early days of a conflict and the ones that pose the most immediate danger of a breakthrough. To focus too much on a more distant threat when one closer at hand is already arguably overwhelming would be sheer folly. We must take great care not to incur a strategic deficit by building for the desirable at the expense of the essential.

A third, and at least equally dangerous, strategic pitfall to the current evolution of Deep Attack concepts exists. This is the tendency of some to speak as if emerging technologies offer an opportunity to substitute deep conventional capabilities for theater nuclear forces. Technologists, in particular, favor such an approach by noting the growing accuracy of delivery systems and the increased lethality and area coverage of conventional munitions. Moreover, many defense analysts are growing disenchanted with the utility and survivability of battlefield nuclear weapons and insisting that they be eliminated wholly or in part from Alliance inventories. Together, these trends, whether intended or not, appear to argue for some level of substitution of conventional munitions for theater nuclear weapons.

Unfortunately, such a change fails to address the broader strategic requirements of Flexible Response. Conventional munitions have and will continue to become more militarily effective against many targets that were formerly vulnerable only to nuclear weapons. But the fact is, theater nuclear weapons have always had a greater purpose than military effects on the battlefield; they have been a means for achieving political results. Theater nuclear weapons threaten escalation of the conflict to a level where the costs and risks of continued aggression are clearly disproportionate to perceived gains. No matter how military effective conventional munitions may become—and they are not yet nearly so effective as nuclear weapons—they simply cannot convey those risks.

On the other hand, the utility of battlefield nuclear systems is clearly suspect. But this is not because conventional weapons are able to replace them. The problem with battlefield nuclear systems is that they are not a credible means of threatening a NATO "first use." First, given the tactical circumstances likely to provoke an Alliance resort to nuclear weapons, battlefield systems will likely prove more devastating to territory and values of the Alliance than to those of the WTO. The FRG, in particular, has been adamant that the destructive consequences of nuclear escalation not be confined to NATO's territory. For that reason Germany has supported an improvement in longer range nuclear systems. Second, given the necessity for continuing political control of nuclear weapons, in war and peace, and the consequent restrictive release procedures, doubt has increased over whether battlefield systems are sufficiently responsive to threaten the mobile target arrays against which they are aimed. Finally, NATO's political authorities have long recognized that the use of battlefield nuclear weapons alone may not achieve either the military or the political ends sought in an Alliance "first use" of nuclear weapons.

However, we must recognize that, whatever the inherent difficulties, battlefield nuclear systems have performed a critical function. They have forced WTO forces to operate dispersed in a "nuclear scared" posture. Despite the promised development of drastically improved conventional munitions, nuclear systems still offer greater damage capabilities. Without the threat of short range battlefield systems, opposing forces would be able to concentrate with far less vulnerability, thus aggravating NATO's conventional defense problem. Moreover, these tactical nuclear systems constitute NATO's last remaining (though now dwindling) measure of nuclear superiority. They serve a vital role in deterring the Soviets from using their expanding nuclear arsenal.

Implications for NATO Strategy

Several implications emerge. First, NATO's conventional and nuclear capabilities are not separate entities but synergistic components of an effective defense posture. They are not substitutable, and deficiencies in one cannot be compensated for by improvements in the other. For that reason, conventional Deep Attack operations must be recognized as complementary, rather than as an alternative, to proposed nuclear "first use" options that rely on similar emerging weapons developments.

One such "first use" option is to direct NATO's longer range nuclear systems toward the disruption and destruction of Soviet operational and strategic follow-on echelons in transit deep in Pact territory before commitment to the forward battle. Such an option is politically useful because it would convey clearly to the Soviets NATO's ability to deny the WTO its war aims; it would also threaten subsequent and more dangerous escalation of the conflict should hostilities continue. Further, such an option meets the demanding criteria for a NATO "first use": it yields a potentially significant military return to communicate the seriousness of NATO's purpose; it signals a willingness to escalate further; and it provides for both central political control and military responsiveness of nuclear options. Finally, given Alliance deployment of Pershing II and ground launched cruise missiles (GLCM) and completion of program improvements to C^3I, NATO can achieve such a capability relatively soon.

The second implication is that NATO cannot afford to dispense with the capability to target with nuclear means the forward attacking echelons of WTO forces. This does not mean that obsolescent weapons could not be removed from Alliance inventories, or that artillery-fired atomic projectiles are necessarily the most effective means of accomplishing the objective. It does mean, however, that NATO must retain a full spectrum of nuclear capabilities to hold at risk the entire depth of attacking forces in order to assure their dispersal.

DOCTRINAL IMPLICATIONS
OF DEEP ATTACK CONCEPTS

The two specific proposals for Deep Attack under discussion in the Alliance, the US Army's AirLand Battle doctrine and the SHAPE Follow-on Force Attack concept, are similar in several respects. Both recognize the significance of the Soviet forces echeloned in depth; both recognize the importance of seeing and attacking in depth; both recognize that airpower is critical for this purpose; and both recognize that this air interdiction must be more closely orchestrated to affect the ground battle. Despite these similarities, however, the two approaches are surprisingly different, both in their underlying assumptions and in their implications.

Distinctions Between the Two Concepts

Origins and purposes. The two approaches reflect their differing origins, the differing concerns of their originators, and the differing parameters within which they were developed. AirLand Battle was developed by the US Army, with Air Force participation, for corps level and below; its purpose is to enable US forces to defeat in battle a technologically equal, numerically superior opponent anywhere in the world. Implicit in AirLand Battle doctrine is the concern that, to defeat even first echelon opposing forces, US forces must alter their approach to warfare by stressing maneuver and fighting in depth. The SHAPE concept, on the other hand, was prepared by an integrated Alliance headquarters. It deals solely with the problem of the opposing forces' reinforcing echelons theater-wide, recognizing that corps will fight according to their various national doctrines.

Allocation of airpower. AirLand Battle doctrine recognizes that a commander must be able to detect and delay or disrupt opposing forces echeloned in depth that could interfere with his operations against the enemy's first echelon. The doctrine requires that a corps strive to maintain surveillance of an area large enough to give 96 hours notice of approaching significant enemy forces; the corps must be able to influence those opposing forces up to 72 hours away from the main battle.[18] With these capabilities, the corps commander is to plan and execute battle actions to wrest the initiative from the attacking enemy force. As this planning-execution window is compressed, the difficulties and risks associated with seizing the initiative will increase accordingly. In the European theater, this 72-hour window, plotted on a map as the corps area of influence, could extend as much as 150 kilometers forward of the main battle.[19]

Some of the key procedural problems for implementing AirLand Battle in NATO are allocation of battlefield interdiction sorties down to corps and below; recognition of an area of influence beyond the Fire Support Coordination Line (FSCL), in which these sorties would be available to supplement organic corps Deep Attack systems; and early allocation of numbers of sorties to enable full integration of airpower into the planning of the ground force.

Current procedures allow for the first and are beginning to take cognizance of the second, but have made little progress in the third area. This notion of early commitment of significant air interdiction forces runs counter to the notion of centralized control of airpower and its dispatch *en masse* to the most crucial portion of the theater. Indeed, this conflict poses a key difficulty in the full implementation of AirLand Battle as it was originally conceived.

Offensive air support, including close air support, battlefield air interdiction, and reconnaissance, can be allocated down to corps level.

The ground commander's area of responsibility forward of the close battle normally ends at the Fire Support Coordination Line, approximately 25 kilometers forward. Beyond this distance, targets are the responsibility of the air component commander, though some measures are now in process to assure that air interdiction of targets to depths of 70–100 kilometers beyond the front line of engaged forces will be coordinated with the ground commander. However, procedures for planning centralized daily apportionment and allocation of air resources at the air component command and subordinate air operations centers are time-consuming. Therefore, procedures have not been developed to allocate the critical battlefield air interdiction sorties far enough in advance. This means that commanders at corps level and below have not been able to adequately integrate the principal means of deep attack—airpower—into their plans. Instead, they have been able to do little more than request air reconnaissance and air attack of certain targets. The commander generally does not know if he will receive such support until a few hours before the battle.

The SHAPE concept, on the other hand, requires no new allocation procedures. It was designed to take advantage of the very centralized air allocation procedures that cause difficulty for AirLand Battle.

Thus, there is this disjunction between AirLand Battle and the SHAPE concept: AirLand Battle thrives on the early allocation of airpower to support the ground commander, a process that reduces the extent of centralized control and application; the SHAPE concept, however, plans for more traditional use of airpower through centralized air allocation and application theater-wide. This disjunction has profound implications for how the ground war can be fought.

Contrasting Implications

Maneuver versus attrition. AirLand Battle posits maneuver by forces up to division size to seize the initiative and defeat forward enemy forces. To do this, however, the corps must have some assurance that the enemy's echeloned follow-on forces will be prevented from interfering with that maneuver long enough to allow a reasonable prospect of defeating the enemy's first echelon. Without some increased confidence that required air assets will be available to support the ground battle, it will be even more difficult and risky for the corps to assume the initiative. In this context then, the disjunction between AirLand Battle and the SHAPE concept in the allocation and application of airpower reflects the tension between a doctrine that recognizes a need to maneuver and one that takes a more traditional (firepower and attrition) approach to the battlefield.

Warfighting versus deterrence. Alternatively, the disjunction may be viewed as a conflict of focus. At corps level and below, the focus is necessarily on warfighting; the foremost consideration must be to prevail in battle against attacking Pact forces. At NATO and region levels, the focus has been on deterrence; the Alliance must "persuade" the Soviets to call off the attack, either because they cannot win or because they cannot afford the costs of winning.

The Army's doctrine is based on the conclusion that maneuver is essential to defeat the Pact's first tactical echelon, and that this will require greater synchronization of air interdiction with ground forces than current procedures envision. But at the strategic level, air interdiction is necessarily the primary means short of nuclear exchange for attacking the Pact rear; therefore, it is an essential element of intrawar deterrence, whose contribution exceeds any materiel damage inflicted. While this deterrent perspective does not rule out greater synchronization of air and ground forces, it does constrain the amount of air resources that can be allocated to the support of ground forces. It also argues for the preservation of the centralized allocation of air resources so that airpower can be massed more easily to support theater requirements and priorities.

Immediate versus delayed impact. A third difference between these two Deep Attack concepts is the time each requires to have significant military (vice political) effect. In this context, the AirLand Battle implies a near term impact through the synchronization of air and ground forces against relatively close opposing formations. Conversely, the SHAPE concept, though currently limited by the combat radii of some NATO attack aircraft, may portend greater weight of attack at greater depths to achieve, perhaps, more significant effects at a somewhat later time.

During an acute crisis, more immediate military needs would tend to receive priority. Faced with the choice between the interdiction of opposing forces still more than 3 days from the battle or the staving off of a breakthrough in the Central Region, the commander would presumably opt to trade future security for present survival. This consideration does not negate the desirability of possessing the capability to strike very deep. But it argues for the necessity of developing the most effective procedures and systems for applying airpower to influence the close battle.

Preconflict deterrence. Examination of the preconflict deterrent implications of the two concepts reinforces the foregoing consideration. To be sure, virtually all improvements in NATO capabilities will tend to strengthen the overall deterrent. But the two concepts have somewhat different impacts on what might be called the crisis stability of the deterrent. Insofar as the capability for deep interdiction is improved, Pact risks in a "bolt from the blue" or limited mobilization attack will be increased. Presumably, this will reduce Pact incentives to attack. But the reduction in Pact incentives may not be as strong in the case of a full mobilization attack. For such an attack, the Pact could bring forward its major formations before the onset of hostilities, negating the full impact of a Deep Attack concept. AirLand Battle, however, would be significant against either a limited or a full mobilization attack because it threatens the destruction of the opposing force echelon in contact.

Impact on NATO doctrine. Finally, we must note that since AirLand Battle doctrine was not designed specifically for the NATO context of separate national corps, its implementation within the Central Region poses unique problems. These problems are distinct from those of implementing the SHAPE concept. For example, if other nations do not employ the concept of an area of influence forward of the main battle, then the development of deep intelligence may be asymmetrical despite the best efforts at inter-Allied intelligence sharing.* Also, the air allocation system may find itself in the dilemma of either taking special cognizance of interdiction requests from US corps—normally viewed as a suboptimization of airpower—or frustrating the very procedures most likely to employ airpower to its fullest effect. Together, these considerations suggest that AirLand Battle may constitute a form of doctrinal encroachment on the procedures of the other national corps unlike that previously experienced.

---

*The development of intelligence is a function not only of raw data, but also of the will and desires of the commander. Despite increased quantities of raw information as a consequence of new technology and centralized distribution systems, intelligence staffs at all echelons still must analyze, refine, and interpret the data. If some corps concentrate on detailed interpretation of data out to depths of 100–150 kilometers while others focus only on the opposing forces in contact, then the clarity with which second echelon enemy units are detected and tracked will vary significantly among the various corps. This means that Army Group must work to compensate for the lack of attention-in-depth by some corps, or else those corps must change the focus of their intelligence efforts to "see" deeper. Without these compensating measures, commanders at Army Group level and above will receive relatively detailed information on enemy second echelon forces opposite US corps but sparse information on second echelon forces opposite some other national corps. This "asymmetrical" intelligence would inevitably be harmful to effective coordinated operations above corps level.

Reconciling the Two Approaches

Must we choose between these distinct approaches? Should both proceed independently? Can they in some way be combined? The Air-Land Battle and SHAPE concepts seem to have both complementary and competitive aspects. Certainly their differing implications with regard to warfighting versus deterrence, the time periods required for military impact during conflict, and preconflict deterrence appear mainly complementary. But the actual wartime allocation of resources for their various purposes might be competitive. And the difference in the implied locus of control of air assets implies alternative approaches to warfighting that are definitely competitive. The tendency of the AirLand Battle doctrine to infringe on other national corps-level doctrines also requires careful consideration.

These complementary and competitive aspects may be examined against three obvious standards. First, can the two different approaches be made procedurally compatible, so that the theater commander may employ either or both simultaneously? Second, can AirLand Battle be fitted into the NATO national corps approach as one nation's battle doctrine? Third, is the military hardware to implement these approaches similar and compatible, or will the theater commander's flexibility in wartime be curtailed by procurements underway today?

Procedures. At present, the centralized daily air allocation procedures clearly restrict the employment of AirLand Battle in Europe. Fortunately, efforts appear to be underway in US circles to deal in part with the air allocation issue. Army and Air Force authorities coordinated a modification of existing air allocation procedures, entitled "Joint Air Attack of the Second Echelon," in December 1982. Under these modified procedures, a Battlefield Coordination Element would operate at the Tactical Air Control Center to prioritize the Army air interdiction requests and insure Air Force appreciation of ground maneuver requirements.

This modification and the recent Air Force decision to endorse Air-Land Battle doctrine represent very positive steps. But we still must transform these agreements into operating procedures within the theater and demonstrate their adequacy, especially their timeliness. In particular, various types of early allocation systems need to be explored carefully. These systems should aim at providing the flexibility to balance US doctrinal requirements at corps level and below with Alliance operational necessities at Army Group level and above.

Doctrine. Only initial measures have been taken to examine the significance of the doctrinal encroachment problem within NATO. The continuing discussions of doctrine at various national, service, and field command levels, should carefully explore the area of influence concept and revised air allocation procedures in the context of European exercises and follow-on discussions. In particular, US corps initial areas of influence should be developed based on both general guidelines and specific terrain features, road nets, and enemy capabilities; how these areas will affect other national corps should be examined.

Another area for attention is the development of intelligence forward of the FLOT in the sectors of non-US corps. Compensatory efforts at Army Group or ATAF level may be required to assure a balanced interpretation of the battlefield beyond the Fire Support Coordination Line.

Finally, we should analyze representative ground maneuver plans with regard to available air interdiction support. We must strike the right balance between providing adequate air interdiction to support the ground commander's scheme of maneuver and assuring that air allocation achieves the most decisive effects theater-wide. As yet, it is too early to determine whether the SHAPE and AirLand Battle approaches can be harmonized to achieve this balance.

Materiel. The two approaches diverge somewhat in their implications for development and acquisition of materiel. Both are somewhat ambivalent with respect to the extent of their reliance on anticipated technological advancement and future procurement. The SHAPE approach requires area surveillance, target acquisition, and attack systems of somewhat greater range while AirLand Battle does not require systems capable of the longer ranges. But AirLand Battle might entail greater attention to tactical C^3, ground mobility, and logistic preparation of the battlefield to support more maneuver oriented warfare and greater air-ground synchronization.

Although both AirLand Battle and the SHAPE concept claim to be viable with current weapons and technologies, official and press discussions of them constantly refer to the opportunities afforded by enhanced technologies. Most of these references are to area surveillance, target acquisition, and attack systems still in development and not expected to be available in significant numbers for another 5 to 10 years. Moreover, very complex developments in all functions—surveillance, information processing and dissemination, munitions, and weapon systems integration—must come on line successfully before their synergistic effect provides the anticipated quantum leap in operational capability. And this increased capability is required for some of the advanced concepts of Deep Attack (especially those involving attacks against units as opposed to fixed facilities) to work to full effect. Given the procurement costs, technological uncertainties, time lines, and interservice issues involved, it is a high-risk force development process.

One of the greatest dangers is becoming too enchanted with the future potential of emerging technology. We must continue procurement of proven systems and incremental upgrades necessary to carry us through until new systems are available; and we must not build current plans, strategy, and tactics as though potential capability already exists.*

The materiel and force development implications of AirLand Battle and the SHAPE concept are competitive but not necessarily incompatible. While no choice between these two doctrinal approaches seems otherwise required yet, we must, at this early stage in the development of Deep Attack systems, consider the problem of doctrine and its relationship to force structure and materiel development. We must directly confront the desirability of attacking very deep with non-nuclear systems. Otherwise, we may inadvertently set our sights on capabilities whose expenses and technical difficulties compound rather than ease the more immediate challenge of strengthening NATO's forward defense.

In any event, assuring that systems developed for deep interdiction are capable of addressing immediate crises of the close battle is critical. At the same time, having the capability to see and attack strategic follow-on echelons will be useful. And we will always need intelligence and command and control capabilities to allow timely choices between battlefield needs. What we must avoid at this stage are procedures or procurements that lock us into either approach. Much additional analysis and careful consideration of the strategic and doctrinal implications of the concepts must precede firm choices.

As this review of the implications of the two Deep Attack concepts has shown, the SHAPE and AirLand Battle approaches are at least as distinctive as they are similar. A choice between the two at this juncture would obviously be premature. However, the most careful consideration of their differing implications, and consequent measures to harmonize these approaches, is warranted now. Otherwise, NATO may find itself less interoperable and rationalized a decade hence than it is today, with

---

*Key technology and development programs are treated in some detail in appendix A.

enormous resources having been invested in measures lacking the flexibility to meet the most urgent problems of the Alliance in crisis or conflict.

THE SOVIET DIMENSION

The open press here and abroad has given AirLand Battle, the SHAPE concept, and Deep Attack technologies prominent treatment. Undoubtedly, the concepts will have excited considerable attention among Soviet defense planners. This chapter examines these developments from the point of view of a Soviet planner assessing their implications for his own forces and doctrine. It identifies current Soviet force development trends and possible future countermeasures relevant to the two concepts, evaluates their potential effects, and reaches conclusions regarding likely Soviet actions and their consequences for the WTO.

Soviet Perception and Assessment

The Soviets are likely to see the AirLand Battle doctrine as a US attempt to move away from an essentially linear, attrition oriented defense. They will see it as emphasizing offensive action and maneuver warfare, and as an attempt to move the focus of combat action into East European (Warsaw Pact) territory. They may see little new, however, in the concept of deep attacks by air and missile forces—something that has characterized NATO operational planning for many years. AirLand Battle's emphasis on offensive maneuver and Western debate over its role in an essentially defensive alliance could heighten Soviet concerns about the possibility of NATO ground maneuver forces attacking through gaps in Pact lines to engage second echelon forces moving in more vulnerable formations.

The Soviets almost always credit the United States and NATO with capabilities that actually are only in some early stage of consideration or development. They also credit the United States with far greater capability to work its will in NATO than it usually has. Therefore, although Soviet analysts probably will recognize important limitations in US and NATO capability to implement Deep Attack concepts fully in the near term, they will probably take AirLand Battle doctrine and Deep Attack seriously and, in some cases, exaggerate both the intent and the capabilities involved.

In terms of its immediate impact, the Soviets probably will see a substantial gap between the newly published US doctrine and current theater-wide Alliance capability. The Soviets could reach the following conclusions:

- Because the ability to seriously delay or degrade Pact second echelon forces (as opposed to damaging fixed targets) using conventional weapons is based substantially on target acquisition, command and control, and weapon systems that have not yet entered US inventories, it is a doctrine that, for the present, even US forces have only limited capability to carry out. In addition, differences among the capabilities and doctrines of NATO air forces will further impede implementation of Deep Attack concepts aimed at integrating the interdiction campaign and the close battle.

- Because NATO forces have few operational reserves and are thinly spread along the entire front, NATO will not have the forces necessary to conduct large-scale maneuver attacks into the Pact rear areas. Pact forces, given their size and depth, probably can deal effectively with the smaller-scale attacks that NATO could mount.

- Because AirLand Battle is, for the present, a unilateral US doctrine applicable to corps level and below, it could not radically alter the character of battle along the entire front, which is manned predominantly by forces of other nations, for some time.

Nonetheless, the Soviet response will likely be ambivalent. Just as others do, the Soviets tend to interpret US and NATO military developments from the perspective of "worst case" assessment. Whether this is because they believe the worst case may occur or because the approach offers them leverage in extracting the maximum share of resources from their own leadership and from their WTO allies is not known. We are likely, therefore, to see public Soviet expressions of concern and, at the same time, expressions of confidence in their continuing ability to deal NATO "aggression" a "crushing defeat." We will have to discern the real impact of these new US and NATO initiatives from changes, or lack of changes, in ongoing WTO force development efforts.

The Soviets likely will conclude that they still, for the present, possess decisive advantages on the battlefield. These advantages stem from the considerable numerical superiority they continue to enjoy, coupled with recent advancements in the technology and structure of their fielded forces and what they regard as the superior moral and fighting qualities of their troops. Thus, they probably will not see any urgent need to alter radically their ongoing efforts to modernize equipment and improve their force structure.

In the long run, however, the WTO probably sees AirLand Battle, Deep Attack concepts, and especially several important new Western technologies as very threatening developments. And they are likely to adjust operational planning, force development, and preparation of the battlefield to meet the challenge of evolving Western doctrine and technology. The Soviets are likely to be particularly concerned about the potential for new doctrine using new technology to destroy large armored formations anywhere on the battlefield, shallow or deep. This would defeat the mainstay of their strategy: the powerful armored columns essential to a high tempo of attack, quick breakthrough, and deep exploitation.

The Soviets are likely to mount a major political-propaganda campaign. They will aim to gain time and perhaps forestall general NATO acceptance of the new doctrine and acquisition of at least some of the new weapons technology. They will also try to create opportunities to exploit politically the inevitable dissension within NATO that attends even modest reexamination of programs, plans, or strategy. This effort probably will fall within the overall context of the Soviets' continuing campaign to forestall deployment of new NATO intermediate range nuclear forces. It will focus on what the Soviets will characterize as a renewed and expensive arms race, the destabilizing effects of the doctrine and the new technology, and the potential—according to the Soviets—for raising (rather than lowering) the potential for war and its ultimate escalation to the nuclear level.

Current Trends and Possible Countermeasures

Both AirLand Battle and the SHAPE concept depend considerably on attacks against deeply echeloned WTO forces in order to gain battlefield advantage. Both also seek advantage through closer integration of this interdiction effort with the close battle involving first echelon forces. And both recognize that for the foreseeable future NATO air forces will constitute the principal means for such attacks.

Both approaches seek to achieve their effect principally by isolating first echelon enemy forces on the battlefield. This will maintain a combat ratio between engaged forces that will not allow the WTO to maintain the high tempo of attack and the early decisive breakthrough that its strategy demands. With this in mind, there are four generic categories of response, any one or combination of which would work against both AirLand Battle and the SHAPE concept.

Add combat power to the first echelon. The Soviets could increase the combat power of their first echelon in one of three ways. They could reallocate units from the second echelon (i.e., place more divisions forward); they could increase the strength of existing units across the board through changes to organization and equipment; or they could place more Soviet, vice East European, divisions in the first echelon.

Considering current WTO organization and operational doctrine, 20–25 divisions probably would be in the first echelon of an attack against NATO's Central Region.[20] Almost half of these divisions are likely to be East European. Analysis of the terrain in Western Europe, however, suggests that this region would support well over 30 divisions in the first echelon. To increase the combat power of their first echelon by at least 20 percent, therefore, the WTO need do little more than change operational plans. This option is a relatively quick fix. The forces are available in the more than 50 WTO divisions already located in Eastern Europe in peacetime; so no more forces from the USSR would necessarily be required, and the WTO would suffer no substantial mobilization or movement time penalty.

Alternatively, the Soviets could put more of their own divisions in the first echelon. Soviet divisions are substantially more powerful than those of their East European allies; they have more modern equipment and heavier tables of organization and equipment. This option, however, would necessitate some advance movement of divisions from the western USSR.

Adding combat power to the first echelon would impose some penalties on the WTO. It would require greater concentration of forces than current Soviet doctrine regards as prudent when faced with the prospect of nuclear escalation. It would put more WTO forces within range of the bulk of NATO's weapons. It would boost NATO's aircraft sortie generation capability due to reduced turn-around time, and would enhance NATO's ability to avoid WTO air defenses by using stand-off weapons. It also would complicate the WTO logistic problem and probably would force the Soviets to revise their existing efforts to make advance battlefield preparations for routes of advance, logistic stocks, and so forth. Finally, it would require substantial reworking of plans for employment of second echelon forces—in essence, a fairly fundamental review of operational concepts.

Another way to increase the first echelon's combat power is to field more capable weapon systems or make organizational changes that add more weapons to existing units. Indeed, the WTO has been doing both in the past few years and might be able to increase their efforts in this regard.

The Soviets have a continuing, dynamic program to modernize their ground forces, and they give priority to their forces in Central Europe. In the past few years, the Soviets have added a new generation of tanks and have substantially modified earlier generations. They also have fielded new towed and self-propelled artillery (much of which is likely to be nuclear-capable), substantial numbers of infantry combat vehicles, a new generation of antitank weapons, and close support aircraft and helicopter gunships.[21] The Soviets' East European allies, however, are modernizing much more slowly. This could cause significant weaknesses in the WTO combat forces opposite NATO's Central Region, especially if—as seems likely—the Soviets rely on Polish and Czech forces for the bulk of the combat power in the north and south, respectively.

The Soviets also have been modifying the organization of their ground forces in Central Europe. For example, the Soviets have recently increased the infantry and artillery components in armored units; and they appear to be increasing the number of tubes in at least some artillery batteries.[22]

Decrease time required to commit second echelon. A second way for the WTO to respond is to decrease the time required to commit second echelon forces. One development in this regard may be the creation of what the WTO calls an Operational Maneuver Group (OMG). The OMG appears to be a direct descendant of what in World War II was called an "operational group." Tank and mechanized "corps"—in reality, reinforced divisions—were assigned top commanders and given the best equipment; then they were used to strike quickly and deeply into the enemy rear.

Today's OMG appears to be a tailored combat formation of division or corps size, created out of the existing order-of-battle. It is intended to be highly mobile and more survivable and self-sustaining than other units. An OMG would be a heavily armored force reinforced with artillery, air assault elements, and aviation. It would follow closely on the heels of the first echelon and would be committed early, either to assist the first echelon or to get into the NATO rear area. Once in the NATO rear, the OMG's mission would be to seize important objectives, destroy operational reserves, interfere with command and control, and interrupt whatever NATO mobilization and reinforcement efforts were under-way.[23]

Improve counter-air capabilities. Counter-air improvements, or the ability to interrupt air-ground coordination through physical and electronic attacks on C^3I systems, would also affect either AirLand Battle or the SHAPE concept because both depend on NATO's offensive air capability. As noted earlier, the WTO hopes to neutralize NATO airpower by conducting a series of theater-wide strategic air operations against NATO airfields, air defenses, nuclear storage, and command and control. Although anticipating heavy losses, they expect to cripple NATO airpower. And with the air reserves available from the USSR, they expect to be able to deny NATO the air superiority it requires to compensate for insufficient ground forces.

The Soviets are likely to continue, and could even increase, their recent emphasis on improving ground attack and close support fighters. In addition, the Soviets have a large and currently modernizing force of tactical ballistic missiles capable of attacks against NATO airfields and defensive missile sites, and the command and control centers so essential to planning and synchronization in both the AirLand Battle and SHAPE concepts. With both the improved fighters and the ballistic missile force, the Soviets could challenge NATO's ability to muster the number of interdiction strikes envisioned by either concept. This would be especially critical if the bulk of NATO aircraft capable of interdiction are tied up for several days trying to gain air superiority.

The Soviets have broadly reorganized their theater air defense structure. The reorganization more closely integrates the forces and operations of their strategic and tactical air defense units. They have an air warning and control system (AWACS) aircraft in advanced development, are fielding true look-down/shoot-down radars on some interceptors, have begun to field a new generation of surface-to-air missiles (SAMs), and are assigning more SAMs to protect their maneuver units. They also have an anti-tactical ballistic missile system in development. All of these will make penetration—especially deep penetration—of WTO airspace more difficult and costly.

Prepare the battlefield. The WTO also could do several things to facilitate rapid movement forward, support of forward echelons, defense of the rear area, and quick recovery from interdiction damage. For example, additional engineer units and prepositioned bridging and road construction and repair equipment and supplies would facilitate rapid and more dispersed movement and recovery from damage. Other measures could include advance preparation of road or rail nets to by-pass choke points; advance preparation of river banks to accept rapid construction of alternate bridge crossings, perhaps in conjunction with nearby concealed stocks of bridging equipment; preparation of fords to facilitate crossing by vehicles with amphibious capability; and preparation of buried tactical pipelines to move high volumes of petroleum, oil, and lubricants (POL).

Effect of Trends and Countermeasures

Most US analyses of conventional combat with the WTO in NATO's Central Region have consistently shown outcomes unfavorable to NATO. Conventional WTO assaults lead to early reverses. The reverses require NATO to use nuclear weapons to redress tactical losses, prevent decisive breakthroughs, and demonstrate Alliance resolve to use all necessary means to defend against WTO aggression.

The early reverses seen by these analyses, and the subsequent escalation to use of nuclear weapons, are brought on by the inability of NATO's forward defense. That defense cannot match the combat power of the WTO first echelon divisions and their rapid reinforcement by closely following second echelon divisions and armies. Lacking large operational reserves of its own, NATO's quick loss of the first echelon battle is potentially catastrophic and requires immediate escalation. This conventional force inadequacy weakened the conventional leg of the triad of Flexible Response. Coupled with an increasingly unfavorable balance of theater nuclear forces and parity in US and Soviet strategic nuclear forces, this inadequacy threatened the very fabric of NATO's deterrent strategy.

Analyses of this sort led US and NATO planners to seek improvements at all levels, including some means to avoid such early losses requiring escalation. The analyses showed that WTO second echelon forces must be prevented from quickly reinforcing the first echelon. If this could be done, recent NATO gains in weaponry, command and control, air defense, and sustainability, coupled with good leadership and tactics, might enable NATO to hold its own *against the first echelon* and establish a coherent defense. New analyses incorporating AirLand Battle doctrine showed a *decent prospect* for success in the first echelon, but by no means *certain* success. It remained a dicey battle.

Thus, any WTO trends or countermeasures that increase the combat power of the WTO first echelon, unless matched by equivalent improvements in NATO's first echelon, will likely diminish the efficacy of either the AirLand Battle doctrine or the SHAPE concept. NATO must view with concern the recent changes in the organization and equipment of Soviet divisions and combat support units in Eastern Europe. These developments are leading to substantial increases in the combat potential of these divisions. And these divisions are opposite what will likely be the decisive theater of combat—NATO Central Region. Further, if the WTO were to increase the number of divisions committed to the first tactical echelon—which, as shown above, could be done by reallocating *existing* forces before reinforcement from the western USSR—NATO's forces could be quickly overwhelmed. Neither AirLand Battle nor the SHAPE concept would be effective.

Other countermeasures could be equally damaging to the new concepts. The Operational Maneuver Group's location close to the battle area, its considerable combat power, and its ability to move forward rapidly, make timely interdiction more difficult. This calls into question some of the underlying assumptions of time and distance in both AirLand Battle and the SHAPE concept.

Soviet counter-air capability, as well as offensive air capability, has grown in the past several years. As a result, NATO air forces will be tied up and used up in the counter-air battle, especially in the first critical days of the theater campaign. The very likely continuation of this trend is another matter of considerable concern. US and NATO aircraft modernization, deployment of the AWACS system, and improved air-to-air munitions capabilities and stockpiles have relieved NATO somewhat. But all of these have been factored into assessments that showed the near term value of AirLand Battle and the SHAPE concept. NATO hopes for more improvements through more effective reinforcement from the United States, better air-to-ground munitions, improved stand-off capability, and better battlefield surveillance and target acquisition capabilities. These hopes, however, depend on programs that either are far short of effective implementation (such as reinforcement aircraft bed-down and cross-servicing capabilities) or will not come to fruition for several more years (such as advanced target acquisition and second generation "smart" weapons). This is a highly dynamic area of competition, and the efficacy of either of the new concepts depends on the state of the competition when combat begins.

Finally, WTO measures to prepare the battlefield can have a decisive effect on what is otherwise a close calculation. NATO needs the ability to isolate the first echelon battle. Given the large WTO second echelon forces involved and the rigors of the air battle noted above, this ability is by no means certain. Additional WTO measures to facilitate forward movement, support, and rapid recovery from interdiction damage will further stress NATO's capability to make either AirLand Battle or the SHAPE concept militarily effective. Moreover, most of these preparations are especially difficult intelligence targets. If the WTO is particularly thorough in such preparations, they may derive added confidence from this "ace in the hole."

Probabilities for the Future

The Soviets are unlikely to take any dramatic new directions in response to either AirLand Battle or the SHAPE concept for three reasons. First, most of the possible WTO countermeasures against both concepts represent a continuation of trends established over the past decade or more. Second, the Soviets probably do not regard either new concept as an urgent, near term threat. And third, the Soviets seldom make radical changes in the development of their defense programs or doctrine.

What we are likely to see are steady and determined efforts by the Soviets along established lines to improve the combat potential of their weapons and units across the board. This greater combat potential will improve their chances in the first echelon battle and their residual capability after direct combat or interdiction damage. The Soviets also are likely to focus on more offensive counter-air capabilities; improved theater air defenses, probably including accelerated development of defenses against cruise and tactical ballistic missiles; and improved theater infrastructure to facilitate movement and damage recovery.

This is not to say that the overall results of their programs will not be dramatic. A look at the cumulative effect of Soviet military achievements in the past decade shows clearly what a determined, consistent effort can accomplish. The USSR was already ahead of the United States in *numbers* of most weapon systems. In recent years the Soviets have overtaken us in the *technology level* of several fielded weapons and equaled us in many more. Now they are beginning to threaten the former strong US lead in three generic systems critical to both AirLand Battle and the SHAPE concept: fighter-attack aircraft, precision guided munitions, and surveillance and reconnaissance.[24] And the Soviets will continue to strive for and achieve advances in new technologies. They have been substantially outspending the United States in military research, development, test, and evaluation (RDT&E) for many years and are now at double US levels.[25]

Many of the countermeasures discussed here would, however, impose some serious difficulties on the Soviets and their WTO partners. All exact money and manpower from economies that cannot spare either. During the past two decades, the Soviets have achieved a position of considerable strength relative to NATO; they have done this at the cost of economic well-being and consumer needs at home. Therefore, the Soviets probably were looking forward to relatively less need for massive military investments in the next decade. With the notable exception of planning modifications—which, in addition to their relatively low costs, might be the most effective—most of the countermeasures to either AirLand Battle or the SHAPE concept would seem to cost the WTO more than implementation of the concepts would cost NATO. Nonetheless, the past record indicates that the Soviets would pay the price rather than lose a hard-won advantage.

Indeed, the added investment burden on the WTO may prove to be a side benefit of either concept. More pressure by the Soviets on their WTO allies for increased defense spending would further strain an already reluctant alliance. This fact, and the fact of additional costs to the Soviets themselves, could provide added incentives for them to seek relief through arms limitation agreements of mutual benefit. If not, then at least the added strains on the Soviet economy, society, and political system may prove beneficial in limiting the Soviets in some other way, such as reducing their willingness to exploit opportunities that might have large resource costs.

To the extent that either AirLand Battle or the SHAPE concept diminishes the WTO's chances for a quick and decisive breakthrough of NATO's forward defense, deterrence is improved. The Soviets realize that general nuclear war would devastate their homeland as well as all of Europe. They have based their strategy for a war in Europe—a war they probably don't want any more than we do—on three objectives: deter NATO's use of nuclear weapons, overwhelm NATO's forward defense quickly, and bring about the early political collapse of the Alliance. The three are completely interdependent. The first allows the second, the second facilitates the first and the third, the third may preclude the first, and so on. But the key is the second: overwhelm NATO's forward defense quickly.

If the Soviets do not achieve the quick breakthrough that this strategy demands, then they face a serious dilemma. Nuclear weapons offer them no panacea under these conditions; the Soviets would face the same prospect of escalation and consequent devastation that guides their strategy and deters use of nuclear weapons at the outset. A prolonged war of attrition would bring to bear the superior economic, industrial, and manpower potential of the West, open severe cracks in an already reluctant WTO alliance, and invite "periphery pecking" by other powers that have had to endure Soviet arrogance for much of the 20th century.

The Soviets are likely, therefore, to calculate that they must be able to achieve quick victory with conventional weapons if the attempt is to be worth the risk. So long as they cannot be confident of gaining a quick victory, NATO's deterrence efforts remain effective.

CONCLUSIONS

In the past several years, a number of initiatives aimed at strengthening NATO's defenses have emerged, grouped under the heading of Deep Attack concepts. These concepts focus on improving conventional defense by attacking in the enemy's rear to disrupt or delay his follow-on forces, thereby controlling the flow of enemy forces into the battle. Two concepts—SHAPE's Follow-on Force Attack concept and the US Army's AirLand Battle doctrine—have received particular attention.

Strategic Concerns

Alliance deliberations on the political acceptability and military utility of Deep Attack concepts will hinge on their strategic implications. Both the SHAPE concept and AirLand Battle doctrine have come under attack because no strategic rationale has been developed to show how each fits into the existing framework. For NATO, the strategic rationale must be centered on support and reinforcement of the existing Flexible Response strategy. Pursuing Deep Attack concepts that significantly reduce reliance on nuclear weapons creates severe problems for NATO because such a move is viewed as an attempt to "decouple," thereby undermining Flexible Response.

Support for Deep Attack concepts should not be based on the argument that emerging technology offers an opportunity to substitute Deep Attack conventional capabilities for theater nuclear forces. NATO's conventional and nuclear capabilities are not separate entities; they are synergistic components of an effective defense posture. One is not substitutable for the other, and improvements in one cannot compensate for deficiencies in the other.

In the competition for limited resources, first priority must be given to the most dangerous threat to NATO. Currently, that threat is the ability of forward-deployed WTO forces to achieve a quick breakthrough of NATO's forward defenses. Deep Attack concepts, then, must be directed as follows: first, against engaged forces and follow-on forces close to the forward battle; second, against more deeply echeloned forces and targets that become significant somewhat later in the battle; and last, against targets that become significant only in a war of attrition.

Tactical Deep Attack and strategic Deep Attack should be differentiated. Tactical Deep Attack—done with conventional weapons—should concentrate on enemy forces that can support a breakthrough attack and targets key to fighting the ground and air wars. These are generally up to about 150 kilometers behind the line of battle. *It would focus on warfighting*, although it would also enhance the conventional leg of deterrence. Strategic Deep Attack, on the other hand, could be accomplished using theater nuclear weapons. (Strategic Deep Attack can be at closer or longer ranges.) It should be directed principally against key transshipment points and those strategic reinforcing echelons deep in Pact territory. *It would focus on deterrence and, should deterrence fail, limiting war.*

Tactical Deep Attack, then, provides a fertile area for the key linkage between conventional and nuclear strategy. Threatening the area approximately 150 kilometers behind the line of battle and beyond with nuclear weapons will hold strategic reinforcements from the USSR at risk, and it will free conventional resources to concentrate on those WTO forces which are the most serious and immediate threat to NATO's defenses. Limiting conventional Deep Attack to tactical uses adds credibility to NATO's stated objective should deterrence fail: to reestablish NATO boundaries, not to carry the war deep into WTO territory and threaten the Soviet homeland. It provides for intrawar deterrence by denying the WTO its military objectives at the conventional level. And it also, by clearly limiting the operational depth of the war, avoids ambiguous signals and weapons employment that might either give the Soviets cause for deliberate escalation or lead them into use of nuclear weapons under the impression that they were under nuclear attack themselves.

Doctrinal Concerns

There are a number of doctrinal and procedural issues that must be resolved before Deep Attack concepts could be implemented in NATO. The theater commander's need for flexibility to allocate Deep Attack systems, primarily airpower, is most important. The commander must be able either to reinforce the battle at corps level or below (through the mechanism of AirLand Battle) or to destroy massed enemy reinforcing echelons (concentrating Deep Attack systems at theater level).

In practical application, AirLand Battle thrives on early allocation of airpower to support the ground battle; this process reduces the extent of centralized control and application. The SHAPE concept, however, plans for more traditional use of airpower through centralized allocation and application theater-wide; this reduces the corps commanders' planning window and, therefore, their ability to fully synchronize air attack and ground maneuver. This implies that the more closely Deep Attack concepts are tied to the ground forces battle plan, the earlier airpower must be allocated to a specific ground commander.

Although there are obvious differences, AirLand Battle and the SHAPE concept can be complementary. AirLand Battle seeks to integrate airpower with the ground commander's battle plan more closely than does the SHAPE concept. But that should be expected because AirLand Battle is a corps-level doctrine while the SHAPE concept applies more explicitly to theater and region levels. Since they can be highly complementary, we must avoid temptations to choose between the two. Therefore, we must avoid early commitment to procedures or procurements that lock us into either approach to the exclusion of the other.

Soviet Responses

Deep Attack concepts are designed to strengthen NATO's conventional defenses, thereby denying the WTO the quick breakthrough and deep exploitation that its strategy demands. Therefore, these concepts will undoubtedly demand considerable attention from Soviet planners. The Soviets will perceive a substantial gap between Deep Attack concepts and current NATO capabilities to carry out the concepts fully. But they will see both AirLand Battle and the SHAPE concept as potentially threatening in the long run.

The Soviets are likely to orchestrate a public campaign against the new concepts and technology to gain time; to possibly forestall NATO's early acceptance of some aspects of the concepts, and its acquisition of at least some of the technology; and to show dissension in an Alliance that shudders at the mere thought of modifying doctrine or strategy. They probably will do this within the overall context of their existing campaign against NATO's INF initiatives.

The WTO goal will continue to be a rapid breakthrough attack deep into NATO territory, forcing a political collapse of NATO before it can decide to use nuclear weapons. The Soviets will not alter this strategy because of AirLand Battle or the SHAPE concept but will continue efforts to structure their forces to achieve rapid advance rates in combat. WTO members, particularly the Soviets, have made significant conventional force improvements in the past decade; and we are more likely to see continuing efforts in this regard than to see any substantial departure from established trends.

However, the WTO does have some options that could offset the advantages of the new concepts and compensate to some extent for the new technology. The WTO could increase the combat potential of its forward echelons by adding divisions (the terrain could support at least a 20 percent increase), by assigning more Soviet (vice East European) divisions to the first echelon, or by adding more and better equipment to existing divisions. The WTO also could increase the speed and ease with which follow-on forces could move forward and recover from interdiction damage. Some examination of all of these options should be expected, and the WTO likely will adopt at least some of these measures.

WTO strategy is to achieve a quick conventional breakthrough of NATO's defenses and inhibit NATO's first use of nuclear weapons. Any decrease in the WTO's confidence in its ability to carry out this strategy increases the risks to the WTO of a conventional attack against NATO. Thus, unless the Soviets are confident that AirLand Battle and the SHAPE concept will not work, that the new technology will not prove out or will not be acquired in significant numbers, or that they can overwhelmingly compensate for the concepts' combined effects, these developments will enhance deterrence. The Soviets, inclined in any case to be conservative planners, are unlikely to have such confidence.

APPENDIX A
WEAPON SYSTEMS CHARACTERISTICS

The destruction of enemy targets in war involves a complex sequence of events that must be conducted with timeliness and precision. As timeliness and precision improve, lethality becomes great enough to significantly reduce the enemy's ability to fight.

These sequential events may occur in a few short seconds, as in close combat; or they may take hours, even days, with variations in distances and in military and political circumstances. But the basic requirements remain the same.

1. **Detection.** Determining that something of interest is within the area of concern.

2. **Recognition.** Determining what is out there, to include as many characteristics as possible, such as location, movement, size, and vulnerabilities.

3. **Decision to attack.** Determining if and when the target is important enough to warrant expenditure of resources, based primarily on a combination of the threat it poses and target vulnerabilities.

4. **Weapons choice.** Determining which weapons to use, based on weapons availability and capability combined with target vulnerabilities.

5. **Weapons allocation.** Determining source of weapons, based on location, inventories, condition, and comparative capabilities of possessing units.

6. **Weapons transport.** Determining whether the strike will be conducted by surface or air, aircraft or missiles, etc., to put weapons in position to engage the target.

7. **Target acquisition.** Once in the target area, the delivery vehicle must acquire the target to release weapons within their effective envelopes.

8. **Weapons delivery.** The weapons must be released under parameters which allow them to engage the target.

9. **Target destruction.** The weapons must have sufficient lethality, through a combination of accuracy and power, to effectively remove the target as a threat.

Overlaying this sequence of events is the necessity for a command, control, and communication (C^3) system to distribute information vertically and laterally among the actors. Because C^3 takes place at every event in the chain, it is simultaneously the area of greatest potential payoff and greatest potential vulnerability. More than any other factor, C^3 can be responsible for enormous success when conducted well, or disastrous failure when conducted poorly. Ultimately, C^3 is the line through which leadership is exercised, and wars are won through leadership.

Research and development efforts in target detection and destruction requirements are wide-ranging but can generally be grouped into three broad categories: surveillance, information processing and dissemination, and weapons systems and munitions. Most current efforts in the first two categories are being conducted under the auspices of major joint service programs. Weapons systems and munitions are being developed in support of the major joint programs in some cases and independently in others.

The Joint Surveillance and Target Attack Radar System (JSTARS) has combined a number of service-directed efforts. The program aims to meet the Army requirement to find moving targets within the corps area of interest and the Air Force requirement to find moving and fixed targets of enemy second echelon forces.[26]

A common multimode radar system will combine moving target indication, fixed target indicating synthetic aperture radar, and real time weapon guidance capabilities. The high altitude Lockheed TR-1 aircraft will carry the system for the Air Force-wide area surveillance mission. The Grumman OV-1 Mohawk aircraft will carry a less complex version for the Army corps area mission. In addition to the image intelligence gathering mission, both aircraft can be equipped to gather and exploit signal intelligence.[27]

The initial JSTARS is not fully autonomous, but transmits data via data link to automatic data processing (ADP) and tracking hardware in several large vans at corps and theater levels. Decisionmakers in the vans then relay target assignment information via data link to the platform aircraft and to strike aircraft or surface-to-surface missiles. The radar system then continues to provide guidance information to the strikers until they acquire and strike their respective targets.[28]

Later in the decade, when microcircuits with better ADP are developed under DOD's Very High Speed Integrated Circuit and Very Large Scale Integrated Circuit programs, the decisionmaking and targeting processes may be collocated in-flight in a large "command center" aircraft. Such a system would greatly reduce vulnerability to communications monitoring or interference, but at the possible cost of greater exposure of decisionmakers to enemy force.

The Army's primary OV-1 collection platform extends the eyes of the corps. In addition, the Remotely Piloted Vehicle with Target Acquisition/Designated Aerial Reconnaissance System can be cued by JSTARS to extend the eyes of the division and brigade beyond ground line of sight to the full range of division direct support artillery weapons.

The primary attack systems to be cued by JSTARS will be the Air Force Stand-off Attack Weapon and the Army Corps Support Weapons System. These weapons will be powered, guided dispensers, designed to carry a full range of submunitions against armor, personnel, or fixed targets. They will give targeting flexibility, and the "fire and forget" concept will reduce exposure to enemy defenses during delivery.[29]

Weapons under consideration for the Army surface-to-surface mission include the Vought T-22 Improved Lance and the Martin Marietta T-16 Patriot missiles. The Air Force is considering modified forms of these two missiles for the air-to-surface mission, as well as the Brunswick Low Altitude Dispenser and a modified form of the General Dynamics Tomahawk cruise missile. All of these would initially provide a stand-off range of 10 to 20 miles by flying a rocket boosted profile to release terminally guided submunitions over the target with appropriate kill characteristics.[30]

DOD is using an incremental preplanned product improvement (P^3I) approach to developing these weapons. They will start with pure inertial navigation system guidance and advance to more sophisticated systems like the Global Positioning System and JSTARS as conditions allow. The weapons will have modular guidance and control units, separate propulsion units, and a variety of modular payloads. This approach should allow rapid integration of improvements.[31]

Initially, these attack systems will serve a specialized role, concentrating on soft, emitting targets, such as enemy high-threat terminal and battlefield defenses like the SA-6, SA-8, and follow-on surface-to-air missile sites. The Joint Suppression of Enemy Air Defense (JSEAD) program is managing this specialized mission. In the defense suppression role, these weapons will augment the air delivered, long range High Speed Anti-Radiation Missile (HARM) and the short range Sidewinder with Anti-Radiation Missile seeker (SIDEARM), currently under late development and early procurement.[32]

Information processing and dissemination to the right places at the right times ultimately ties the sequential steps together for target destruction, thereby determining the effectiveness of combat power. Two major joint programs and numerous minor joint and service programs pursue these ends.

The Joint Tactical Fusion Program is developing automatic data processing assistance for a common service requirement to reduce/correlate available sensor data into single meaningful events, which can help decisionmakers or intelligence users to reduce tactical uncertainty.[33] The computer science goal is to develop artificial intelligence to the point that "thinking" computers will sort the glut of incoming information, evaluate the data, suggest probable actions by enemy forces, and list the best responses.[34]

After the information is fused, it must be disseminated with necessary decisions, instructions, and amplifications to various users for differing functional applications. The Joint Tactical Information Data System (JTIDS) is the largest development program for this requirement. Information can be transmitted, using verbal, written, and graphic means that are secure and jam-resistant, to receiver terminals small enough for use by fighter aircraft and soldiers in the field. This C^3I development will allow users at all levels to monitor enemy positions as well as the positions and conditions (such as fuel and ammunition state) of other friendly forces in the area. The user can selectively screen his monitoring to eliminate undesired information during critical activities. Included with JTIDS is the Army and Marine Corps Position Location Reporting System (PLRS). This system will automatically provide commanders with near real-time, precise locations of their forces on the battlefield, regardless of terrain, weather, or geographical location.[35]

The Joint Interoperability of Tactical Command and Control Systems (JINTACCS) program is developing standards and testing selected joint service tactical data systems to ensure that they are interoperable and compatible.[36]

The Joint Tactical Communications Program (TRI-TAC) is managing the joint transition of the services from their current tactical analog equipment to a modern digital communication system providing voice, data, and facsimile.[37]

Two major Air Force weapons systems under development are not being managed in direct consonance with the broad-based joint programs but will greatly enhance weapons delivery capability. They are the Surface-to-Surface Airfield Attack Missile (SSAAM) and the Low Altitude Navigation & Targeting Infra-Red System for Night (LANTIRN).

The SSAAM would be used to close enemy runways either before aircraft could launch for attacks on friendlies or while they are airborne, forcing dispersal to much more vulnerable alternate recovery airfields. Candidate ballistic missiles include variants of the US Pershing II, the French M-4, and the Lockheed Axe, which uses the Trident C-4 booster for propulsion. Range would be approximately 350 nautical miles with a 14,000-pound payload. The warhead would contain over 350 kinetic energy penetrator submunitions to be dispensed in a pattern along a runway target. Each submunition would penetrate a runway before detonation to cause an upheaval of the surface, making it time-consuming and difficult to repair. One such submunition has completed the development process by the Air Force under the name "clustered airfield defeat" munition and is being further refined as the "boosted kinetic energy penetration." Circular error probable for the submunitions is 100–150 feet, depending on target range. Dispersal pattern width is 200–500 feet, depending on dispensing altitude.[38] Assuming use of off-the-shelf hardware, development costs are estimated at $500 million, and production could begin within 4 years.[39]

This concept is believed capable of closing all hardened airfields in Warsaw Pact nations within 10 minutes. NATO would gain immediate air superiority while conserving aircraft for other critical missions. It would require no data link and, therefore, would be unjammable. It could be retargeted before launch in less than 10 seconds.[40]

The LANTIRN system, or a Forward Looking Infra-Red system like it, will add a day/night, adverse weather attack capability to single seat aircraft by performing three basic functions:

1. Perform low-level day or night navigation and automatic terrain following, using a Texas Instruments terrain following radar and a Martin Marietta or Ford Aerospace wide field of view imaging infrared sensor.

2. Acquire, identify, and prioritize land targets, based on preprogrammed recognition criteria. Target data is then transferred to the aircraft fire control system, which will launch multiple Maverick missiles against several targets on the same pass.

3. Acquire, automatically track, and laser-designate fixed ground targets, using either FLIR imagery or visual techniques.

The terrain-following radar, FLIR, and tracking/laser-designating technology have been proven in previous systems. But DOD views the target recognizer system as a technically challenging, high-risk item, and it has been classified as an advanced development program. The recognizer has been under competitive development since early in the program, and both systems seem on track. Combined development and initial operational test and evaluation programs in late 1984 could lead to rapid production startup at that time.[41]

In the munitions category, general-purpose bombs will continue to be important and will benefit from more precise fuses plus more sturdy retarding devices, such as the air-inflatable assembly, for low-altitude releases. Glide bomb units will continue in sizes up to 2,000 pounds, with TV, imaging IR, and laser guidance. They will include low-level configurations that climb after release to acquire the target and then dive onto it. Better guidance and shaped-charge explosives will upgrade the AGM–65 Maverick in reliability and lethality.

Various tactical munitions dispensers are under development to deliver submunitions:

1. GATOR Mine disperses mixed antiarmor and antipersonnel devices to wait in the target area.

2. Cluster Bomb Units have combined-effects munitions for real-time attacks against combined armor and personnel targets.

3. Extended Range Antiarmor Munition will dispense "smart" antiarmor submunitions in the target area. When the submunition's acoustic sensor detects an approaching vehicle, it hurls an explosive above the vehicle. An infrared sensor in the explosive detects when it is exactly overhead and fires a shaped charge to create a self-forging projectile aimed at the

heat source. If the IR sensor fails to detect a hot target against which to fire a self-forging projectile, then late in its trajectory the charge detonates in a different manner, producing a shotgun effect useful against personnel and lightly armored targets.[42]

This exploration shows clearly that emerging technology holds great promise for the future in dealing with enemy assaults. But we need to follow this path with prudence.

While the least complex surveillance systems and limited smart munitions are coming on line now, the more complex systems like sophisticated IMINT, weapons system guidance, information processing, and information dissemination are not projected to complete development until the mid-eighties; meaningful deployment will not be until the late eighties. Given the normal failures and time-consuming solutions, plus our track record of delay in search of a more perfect capability, fielding of these systems is doubtful before 1990. An even later date is likely because this modernization, unlike others, requires that all functions—surveillance, information processing/dissemination, and weapons systems/munitions—come on line successfully. Only then will their synergistic effect allow our capability to do anything more than creep ahead at the routine rates of the past.

There is a great danger in this modernization process: we may become too enchanted with the *potential* of emerging technology. First, this may make us fail to continue procurement of proven weapons systems and C³ upgrades to carry us through any war in the meantime. And second, we may build current strategy, plans, and tactics as though the potential capability already exists. We must commit to the new systems today, but only in terms of funds for development and procurement setup. We must not commit *away* from our old systems until the new systems are truly proven capable and reliable, and are fully deployed to all using agencies.

APPENDIX B
COST IMPLICATIONS

Any attempt by NATO to upgrade its defensive posture, whether through modernization or increased force structure, will require economic sacrifices from all nations involved. Such has been the case ever since the Alliance was formed. But in the past, the European NATO countries relied heavily on US leadership and dollars to provide a credible deterrent.

Following World War II, NATO's deterrent posture was based almost exclusively on the US nuclear arsenal, with modest conventional contributions made by NATO countries. At the time this arrangement made good sense since Europeans generally were concerned with domestic economic recovery.

In the 1960s, the picture began to change substantially, at least from the US perspective. Europe had recovered economically and could start sharing more of the burden for its defense. WTO conventional forces became viewed as more of a threat, primarily because of the buildup of forces in the GDR, Poland, and Czechoslovakia. Soviet nuclear forces were expanding and, in the early 1960s, were perceived to be stronger than they actually were. This in turn raised questions about the credibility of the US nuclear forces acting as a deterrent against a WTO attack in Central Europe.

US leadership pushed for a NATO strategy that relied more on conventional defense while still retaining "flexible" options, up to and including a strategic nuclear attack by US forces on the Soviet Union should the WTO attack Western Europe. NATO adopted the Flexible Response strategy (MC 1473) in 1967. The cost of implementing the strategy still fell in large part on the United States. Efforts to coax the Europeans into paying a larger share for their own defense resulted in burden sharing arrangements, particularly with the FRG. The West Germans agreed to offset part of the costs for stationing US forces in the FRG. Another tactic used by the US government was to threaten to withdraw substantial US forces from Europe. The return of limited air and ground forces to the United States in 1968, with the promise of their rapid return to Europe in a crisis, partially carried out this threat.

While these tactics had some effect on the Europeans, they did not cause the Europeans to assume the bulk of the responsibility for their own defense. In the 1970s, the United States continued efforts to reduce its costs for European defense by establishing a series of force goals for all NATO partners. Specific areas of modernization or force building were specified for each NATO country over each of the succeeding 5 years. The primary purpose was to give each nation a series of challenging force goals early enough so they could be included in long term budgeting processes. Some progress was made, but all of the nations continually fell short of the planned force goals. In practice, although nations agreed to the force goals, domestic politics and economics prevented them from meeting those goals.

The conventional force buildup in the early 1970s provided a shell for conventional defense. However, NATO's forward defense lacked credibility because of clearly identified maldeployment of forces and severe shortages in manpower and equipment. In 1977, NATO initiated the Long Term Defense Program to put some teeth into its forward defense posture.

One could argue that all the US initiatives ultimately were designed to force European NATO countries to bear more of the burden for their own defense. But even with these efforts, the United States was successful only in coaxing the Europeans to hold the line in defense spending during the 1970s. This was a victory of sorts because during the same period US defense spending as a percent of the gross national product (GNP) was decreasing.[43]

Generally speaking, during the 1970s, economic conditions were reasonably good for the primary NATO countries. Real GNP growth, while not as high as during the 1960s, was substantial. Unemployment and interest rates were down, and only inflation was considered high by most countries.[44] During relatively good economic times then, the United States was not successful in gaining support from the European NATO countries for any substantial real increase in defense spending as a percent of GNP.[45]

Today the United States has tabled a new initiative to strengthen conventional defenses in Europe. The efforts during the 1970s were deemed insufficient to build a credible forward defense for the 1980s. SHAPE's Follow-on Force Attack concept, according to the United States, will significantly improve conventional defenses and enhance deterrence, making war less likely. Estimates of the concept's cost vary but are roughly $9.5 billion.[46] This amounts to $1 billion for development and $8.5 billion to field and man the systems for 10 years.[47] General Bernard Rogers, SACEUR, has suggested that the concept could be paid for if NATO nations would increase their annual real growth in defense spending from 3 percent to 4 percent for each of the next 5 years.[48]

While spending on defense has been a difficult issue for the West Europeans, it is more acute now because of the prevailing economic conditions in Europe. While the rate of of inflation is decreasing in all nations, interest rates and unemployment have not yet decreased.[49] In fact, most nations, particularly the United States, are running large budget deficits; money continues to be tight and interest rates high, stifling economic growth.

The future does not look much brighter. Predictions are that interest rates will remain high and unemployment will continue to rise, peaking sometime in

1983.[50] Under the circumstances we can expect European NATO countries to attend to domestic economic problems more than defense spending against the Warsaw Pact threat.

The following table shows selected NATO countries' past performance in trying to meet the 3 percent target established in 1979 for annual real increases in defense spending. These figures give further evidence that the Europeans will have great difficulty meeting the 4 percent target.

NATO Defense Spending
Percent Change From Previous Year in Constant Dollars

Country	1979	1980	1981
FRG	1.8	1.9	1.9
Italy	2.6	4.9	−1.2
UK	3.0	2.7	2.1
US	3.4	4.9	5.4

Source: OSD, *Report on Allied Contributions to the Common Defense*, March 1982.

In summary, when economic conditions in Western Europe were reasonably good, European NATO countries had difficulty just holding the line on defense spending. The industrialized West is now in the middle of a deep recession. Major NATO countries are experiencing high unemployment and economic stagnation. Additional revenues are difficult to generate under current economic conditions. European NATO countries are focusing on real domestic issues, not on defense against a Warsaw Pact threat that, as viewed by the Europeans, was never as strong as portrayed by the United States and is weaker today than in previous decades. For the most part, NATO nations have not met their 3 percent goal in real growth for defense spending agreed to in 1979. They do not appear to be in a position to meet the 4 percent goal required to fund the SHAPE concept.

4

ATLANTIC COOPERATION
FOR PERSIAN GULF SECURITY

by

David M. Ransom
Department of State

Lawrence J. McDonald
Lieutenant Colonel, US Marine Corps

W. Nathaniel Howell
Department of State

David M. Ransom, US Department of State, specializes in the Middle East and international relations. Lieutenant Colonel Lawrence J. McDonald, US Marine Corps, was one of the original officers assigned to the Rapid Deployment Joint Task Force. W. Nathaniel Howell, US Department of State, has over 15 years of experience in Middle East affairs and an academic background in Soviet Middle East policy. All three authors are 1983 graduates of the National War College.

INTRODUCTION

Growing differences between the United States and Europe strain NATO. Balances in and between nuclear and conventional weapons, defense costs and disarmament strategies, trade with the Soviets, relations with the Third World, the US security guarantee, and imperfect forms of consultation—these are subjects of discussion that separately and collectively strain NATO's fabric.

Surprisingly, one Atlantic problem—security of the Persian Gulf—that combines elements of all these burning issues receives scant consideration. German Foreign Minister Genscher could even propose an "Overall Western Strategy" [1] in 1982 that never mentioned the Middle East.

Yet the Middle East, particularly the Persian Gulf, is an Achilles heel of the Atlantic community, now and for the foreseeable future. We hardly need to document that Europe would be more directly and immediately affected than the United States by problems in that region. Security in the region should be a central military and political concern because events there can shift the balance of power against the West. [2]

Reasons exist for NATO's failure to adequately consider Gulf security. Other issues crowd the agenda and overload circuits. More fundamentally, however, complicated and deep-seated differences in perspective seem to explain the limited dialogue and the lack of results.

Since 1979, under two administrations, the United States has sought to discuss and forge a common defense strategy with only tepid European response. The United States has, however, focused on defense spending and security rather than the difficult task of coalition building, offering Europeans a role in military cooperation but no input into diplomatic and economic strategy. This focus has preserved US independence in energy matters and on sensitive issues like the Arab-Israeli peace process—a division of responsibility and authority Europeans find unappealing, even dangerous.

Given the failures of the past several years, one may ask whether the Alliance can agree on a coordinated political-military approach to the Middle East. What will move Europeans to assume added costs and commitments to protect vital interests there? What will move the United States to give up a measure of its independence of action in an area of such high stakes to its closest allies?

Two compelling reasons for seeking common ground within the Atlantic community suggest themselves: (1) the United States has invested heavily in a Rapid Deployment Force (RDF) without producing what its own military would term a workable military strategy for the defense of Southwest Asia, and (2) backlash in Congress over NATO's failure to help with the defense of Southwest Asia could produce legislative revolts against proposed US funding and troop levels for NATO. These are serious shortcomings that Atlantic cooperation could substantially remedy. Also, the time has never been better for building a transatlantic consensus. The present oil price collapse reduces pressure on the US and European markets; and the Reagan initiative, which builds upon the Camp David Agreement, provides an opening for a political dialogue.

This essay lays the basis for a discussion, overdue on both sides of the ocean, of Atlantic cooperation for Gulf security. The discussion could produce a broadly shared strategy toward the region, addressing political and energy needs *and* providing a workable contingency plan for defense of vital Western interests. Our focus is on an agenda for military cooperation and related mechanisms for coordination. But other aspects and habits of consultation are no less essential to success.

The outline is simple. We begin with a brief look at why the problem has been viewed so differently and discussed in such a limited way on both sides of the Atlantic. Then we consider Western interests, particularly oil, in the region and threats to those interests, and suggest an overall approach to Middle East policy. Subsequently, we review the development of current US military strategy, both achievements and shortcomings. And finally, we outline an agenda and possible procedures for a coordinated Atlantic effort.

WHERE SHALL THE TWAIN MEET?

The reason why the subject of coordinated policy toward the Middle East has received so little attention is not difficult to discern. The United States has been extremely active, and partially successful, in the diplomacy of the peace process and has sought to retain a free hand in the region. It has recognized that its ability to deal with both Israel and important Arab states is a unique asset. But the United States seems not to have appreciated that this is a wasted asset unless it is able to shape a comprehensive settlement in a reasonable period. The United States has a special relationship with Israel and particular energy, finance, and commercial interests, and it has assumed the burden of "peacemaker." Therefore, the United States has not sought serious consultative relationships with its European allies on the broader aspects of Middle East strategy.

Traditionally, and with particular emphasis since the enunciation of the Carter Doctrine, the United States has sought not only to deter Soviet threats to Gulf stability, but also to limit Soviet influence throughout the region. Efforts to forge a "strategic consensus" to confront Soviet inroads and threats in the Gulf region early in the current administration foundered. Friendly states in the area were not unconcerned about Soviet intentions, but they regarded local threats as a greater and more immediate source of danger. This experience has led to greater US emphasis on resolution of the Arab-Israeli conflict, continuation of which severely limits Arab security cooperation with the United States. However, Washington has continued to hold Europe at arm's length regarding diplomatic planning.

The European governments—insofar as one may disregard differences of view and nuance among them—have approached the Middle East from another tack. Most available commentary in Western Europe concentrates not on defense of the Gulf, but on political, diplomatic, and economic relationships and a resolution of the Arab-Israeli conflict. The tendency is to ignore or play down threats, from the Soviets and others, that are not susceptible to negotiation or blandishments. We cannot be sure whether this tendency reflects conviction or a sense of impotence and risk. But without a doubt, the Europeans have sought, in varying degrees, to distance themselves from US policy they see as closely tied to Israel's current assertiveness and overly focused on the Soviet threat.[3]

Looking at the same set of problems, Europe and the United States have drawn different conclusions and professed to pursue different courses. Europeans have behaved as if the problem of the Middle East and oil access is not a security matter but a social, political, and economic one. They believe that direct Soviet intervention is unlikely and that emphasis on the possibility may exacerbate local instabilities.

Europe, much more than the United States, depends on Gulf oil. And the Middle East is a larger market for European goods than the

United States and Japan combined. Europe's stakes in the region are extremely high; and Europeans appear not to like the odds on defense of the region, particularly when the Soviets would have critical time and distance advantages in any confrontation. Then too, at least some Europeans, contemplating the threat and US responses, may believe the United States will have no choice but to meet a Soviet challenge should it occur.

European efforts, consequently, have been directed toward Euro-Arab dialogue, North-South talks, bilateral oil arrangements, détente with the Soviets, and exploration of a Palestinian option. The United States has tended to see much of this activity as posturing and rationalization of a clear and present danger. And in fact, the Europeans appear to have little to show for their efforts. One European commentator, for example, concedes that European efforts amount to little so far, and "can at best set a pattern for US diplomacy, both complementing American efforts and exerting subtle pressure on the United States . . . one means of by-passing certain constraints on [the] flexibility [of both sides]." [4]

Out-of-area efforts also raise some excruciating questions of Allied military strategy. The US proposals for Gulf defense pose, in another form, all too familiar US-European arguments about flexible and inflexible response, or escalation dominance in an age of parity. US planning for Southwest Asia further skews the balance in Europe against NATO. It suggests, both in the Middle East and in Europe, a lower nuclear threshold. Avoiding that in Europe could mean a weakened commitment to forward defense. Horizontal escalation could involve the European homeland, engaging the US strategic nuclear guarantee. Vertical escalation, given the time and distance advantages of the Soviets in Central Asia and the Caucasus, could lead to quick conventional defeat of US forces in the Gulf. The strategic issue has not been discussed; indeed, it has been studiously ignored.

Before proceeding further, we should note that several structural deficiencies amplify differences between the United States and its allies in perspective and judgment. The Middle East (Persian Gulf) is the first area outside the NATO geographic region to acquire vital importance to the Alliance's well-being and, indeed, its ability to defend itself. Also, on a more mundane level, the problems posed by its security fall between bureaucratic departments in all concerned governments. European and Middle East specialists do not routinely exchange views, either within a single government or among allies. Finally, no forum exists within or outside NATO for sustained attention to such extra-Alliance issues. Thus, when Under Secretary of Defense Robert W. Komer, near the end of the Carter administration, and Under Secretary of Defense Fred Ikle, at the beginning of the Reagan administration, made specific suggestions regarding security cooperation, they addressed the NATO Permanent Representatives, with very little response.

NATO adopted some limited measures in the aftermath of the Soviet invasion of Afghanistan, anticipating an out-of-area contingency for the Alliance. These measures followed US suggestions put forward by Mr. Komer. NATO approved a further, more extensive set of measures in December 1980; but it delayed a full-scale review to permit the incoming Reagan administration to brief the Allies fully on contingency plans for deployment in Southwest Asia. Mr. Ikle gave this briefing, together with a detailed assessment of Soviet capabilities in the region, in the Fall of 1981. The United States urged three steps on the Europeans: (1) facilitate US deployments, which were to constitute the vast majority of forces in Southwest Asia; (2) prepare for some deployments of their own forces; and (3) assume a heavier, compensatory burden in Europe. The United States also sought a public statement of a NATO consensus on the threat and NATO's response, and the development of specific contingency plans.[5]

The European allies have delayed action on all. but the first of these requests. They have asked, instead, for a study of the impact of planned US deployments on NATO defense plans. That impact is, of course, considerable in air, ground, and naval forces, particularly for the US force envisaged for the late 1980s. The study has taken a long time. It is now expected in June 1983 and can perhaps be used in shaping NATO force structure plans for 1983–90. To date, however, this process amounts to little more than talk.

WESTERN STRATEGIC INTERESTS AND VULNERABILITIES

European and US interests in the Middle East are longstanding. But developments of the last decade have combined to raise these interests to questions of strategic importance. While the region has always been regarded as a possible target of Soviet expansion, the dependence of the West and much of the Third World upon Gulf oil is what makes the region's defense vital. In the 1970s, price rises, an embargo, and producer instability dramatically demonstrated Western vulnerability on this score. The collapse of the Shah's regime in Iran and the resulting chaos, local conflict between revolutionary Iran and Iraq, and the Soviet move into Afghanistan in late 1979 underlined the importance of the region and threats to its stability and security. In fact, sudden demands by the Carter administration for European cooperation after the Soviet invasion of Afghanistan and the seizure of the US Embassy in Tehran are what focused the issue squarely for the United States and Europe.

These developments have affected strategic thought. Reflecting one major trend in thought, the Atlantic Council's Working Group on Security Affairs concluded in early 1980,

> The Western nations will have no satisfactory options and no range of action if they have inadequate capability to back up their vital interests with combat forces available to help in the Third World. Indeed, the very existence of such a capability will be a major factor to be weighed by any government deciding on whether or not to risk hostilities over an issue truly vital to the West.[6]

The United States has opted for a strategy of deterrence backed by a serious response capability. This began with the Carter Doctrine and has continued with development of a military deployment capability.

Implicit in all consideration of Gulf security has been a high degree of uncertainty or vagueness regarding the nature of the threat. Apart from palpable threats in the region, the present dichotomy of view between the United States and Europe regarding Middle East strategy bears its own corrosive danger.[7] This threat is perhaps the most overlooked. The United States frequently appears to act alone in both diplomacy and security policy. As we have noted, the arguments that divide the Allies regarding the Middle East tend to deepen over time without corrective action. Untreated, this US-European relationship could drift toward rivalry and disgruntlement. With the high stakes and risks in the Middle East for both the United States and Europe, a growing perception that we are acting at cross purposes would add a substantial, perhaps fatal strain on the Alliance and its ability to preserve a stable world order.

A second order of threats, not dependent upon Soviet instigation but clearly to Moscow's advantage, also could undermine NATO and the Atlantic relationship. Indigenous instability à la Iran, local conflicts exemplified by the Iran-Iraq war, or political decisions to halt oil flows for a prolonged period would be equally disruptive. Remedies for this range of contingencies must be flexible, covering a range of Western and local responses.[8] Military intervention need not be the only or the preferred remedy. But incapability to react militarily, in cooperation with local forces or in response to local invitations, deprives the Western policymaker of a crucial option.

Clearly, a Soviet military move into the region presents the most dangerous, if perhaps less likely, challenge to Western interests and the global balance. We see this as the third threat. In control of the region, the Soviets could deny vital oil supplies to the West or use the threat of denial to force Western political accommodation. Soviet denial or control of Gulf oil supplies would decisively alter the global strategic equation; it would undermine US economic, political, and military leadership and leave the Soviets dominant on the Eurasian land mass.

Direct Soviet invasion may, as many Europeans argue, be highly unlikely; and no Middle East state, however closely tied to the USSR, seems likely to surrender willingly its sovereignty and well-being to the Soviets. But to be prudent, the Alliance must position itself to contest so momentous and adverse a shift—a shift that would lay Europe itself open to paralysis or incapacity for self-defense, except by relatively brief nuclear warfare.[9]

Clearly, the USSR's proximity to the Gulf gives it important potential for access and leverage even without invasion. Aside from Russia's historic urges toward the Gulf ports, relative weakness in this strategic area near the southern extremities of the Soviet empire might be an artificial situation, a circumstance made possible by the presence of great power influence—Britain in an earlier age, the United States today.

One can make a credible case that Moscow has pushed hard, if opportunistically, to carve out a position and establish leverage in the region. Soviet efforts to gain positions in Aden and Afghanistan, Ethiopia and Syria, and Iraq can be viewed in this context. But a master plan driving Kremlin policy is not clear. Whether or not a master plan has existed, Moscow has derived little real influence from its efforts. Relations with Syria are hardly sound and are countered by US relationships with Egypt, Israel, and Saudi Arabia. Soviet fishing in Iran's troubled waters has yielded little to date beyond further estrangement from an independent-minded Iraq. And the Soviet position in Afghanistan is not consolidated.

The Soviets may have concluded, quite sensibly, that acquiring a direct position, enabling them to halt or modulate the flow of oil to Europe and Japan—and shift the global power balance in their favor—would provoke war with the West. If so, the Carter Doctrine and subsequent US military preparations would have been effective in their deterrent role. The Soviets ought logically to calculate that there is a fundamental asymmetry between Western and Soviet interest in the Middle East—the West must have it to maintain its strength, while the Soviets see it only as a means of weakening the United States and its allies. So long, but only so long, as the readiness and will of the West to respond effectively is credible, this equation provides the basis for deterrence.

In any case, the Soviets must recognize that a vital Western pressure point lies tantalizingly close to the south. The Atlantic community must recognize that Moscow's calculation of relative risks is among the many factors that might tempt the Soviets to seek, directly or through surrogates, to squeeze this pressure point. Will a new generation of Soviet leaders be less cautious and yield to temptation, particularly if seizure of the Gulf resources would carry less certainty of global conflict than would an attack on Europe? Could the Soviets see pressuring the West in the Gulf as a way to offset threats to vital Soviet interests elsewhere—a closer Western strategic relationship with China, the disintegration of Moscow's Eastern European empire? And what will the USSR risk should it lose (as Eastern Europe has already lost) its capacity to sustain growth and international commitments without resort to the international oil market? In the future, access to Gulf oil may be critical to the USSR's security and well-being. Melvin Conant, for example, has imaginatively suggested that a Soviet energy plan for itself and Europe might even provide a lever for prying Western Europe from the United States and creating a system of cooperation and accommodation excluding the United States.[10]

How much Middle East oil the Soviets will need, and how soon, are important questions. Conant estimates the total could be 2 MMB/D by 1985. Others have speculated that the Soviets will be prepared to pay a very high price domestically to sustain oil autonomy—an autonomy that is one of their great strategic advantages. Nevertheless, our inability to respond confidently to these fundamental queries underlines both the strategic importance of the Middle East/Persian Gulf and the uncertainties we face regarding Soviet intentions and risk calculations there.

Soviet interest in the oil of the Gulf may be as much an opportunity as a threat, at least in the short term. Assuming they will prefer to have recourse to the international market rather than seize control of one or more producers, their access will have costs for them; perhaps it will also have benefits in terms of Soviet behavior worldwide. We cannot set market prices; Gulf producers will do so. The major producers in the lower Gulf, and possibly the Iraqis, are well disposed toward the West. They would have to set production levels high enough to accommodate Soviet demand in a market where Western economic revival is likely to have eliminated the current glut and some of the softness in spot-market pricing. In such circumstances, the Atlantic community has leverage in protecting the marketing system. It provides the banking system, reserve and transaction currencies, and markets for investment and purchases. But economic cost is only one of the prices the Soviets might be expected to pay. Good behavior, and potentially détente that is indivisible for Moscow as for the West, is another potential cost. To achieve this benefit, and to divert competition into peaceful channels, US and European security cooperation is crucial as a buttress for our regional friends.

ATLANTIC COOPERATION IN GULF SECURITY

The Atlantic community's success over the postwar period owes much to shared perceptions of the military threat to Europe and the free world posed by Soviet might. The Allies concluded decades ago that failure to provide the means for a credible deterrent in Europe increased the possibility of conflict. At a more fundamental level, however, the Alliance sustained its vitality because participants shared, in the main, a concept of the kind of Europe and, indeed, world they sought to build behind its shield. European recovery and prosperity, European unity, a pluralistic international order of independent and responsible states—these goals have been at least as important as military preparedness in animating the Alliance. In fact, would a fundamentally defensive alignment have proved a durable institution if it were not more than an association of individual military capabilities?

The important problems and challenges posed by the question of Gulf security today require similar cooperation and a new focus for the ideas and values integral to Alliance politics. Both the United States and its Allies support the integrity and independence of the friendly states of the region. Leaders on both sides of the Atlantic concede the vital importance of the region and its resources to their strength and the world balance. None of them seeks a conflict with the USSR in that or any other region. And all agree on the importance of supporting stability in the region, including the resolution of destabilizing local conflicts. So there is substantial agreement within the Alliance on which to base a viable security strategy.

Sustained, joint attention to the larger problems of the Middle East has been lacking. But some progress has been achieved in nibbling away collectively at the marginal issues arising from the situation there. The

International Energy Agency (IEA) has analyzed Western energy dependence and options for minimizing the costs and risks in the long run. IEA was instrumental in averting panic at the outset of the Iran-Iraq war. Western banking circles have collaborated to provide liquidity and new loans for countries with severe debt servicing problems. They have also worked together to rationalize national efforts—disinflation in the United States, for example—with international financial flows. Energy conservation and stockpiling have been advanced, with prior consultation, to common advantage. Yet, many marginal differences and doubts remain, which call for closer cooperation if the agenda is to be cleared.

Attention to marginal issues alone, however, will not be sufficient or commensurate with Western stakes in the region. We need nothing less than a broadly shared Western strategy—political, economic, *and* military—to protect the demonstrably vital common interests there. The ability to respond militarily to Soviet or other threats is an unavoidable element of an effective policy. But cooperation will be difficult if some or all of the Europeans feel that some US policies heighten the chances of instability and reduce prospects for cooperation with states in the region. On the other hand, Europeans must be prepared to assume practical responsibilities. Such responsibilities go beyond issuing declarations and principles for the United States to implement, for example, in a Middle East peace process, or implying that resolution of this issue will dissolve threats in the region to Western interests. Furthermore, Europe would seem to have an interest in contributing to a credible deterrent to Soviet or Soviet-inspired moves in the Gulf, seeking to forestall conflict and, if deterrence fails, to limit conflict to the region.

Nothing short of a transatlantic bargain, recognizing the essential trade-offs outlined above, is required to undergird and sustain effective security cooperation in defense of Southwest Asia and Western interests there. For all of its new-found strength and assertiveness, Europe will continue to depend for the foreseeable future on US strength and commitment. It will be dependent not only for the security of Europe, but also for leadership in assuring Western interests in the now-vital Gulf region. The United States, while a global power, likewise needs the cooperation and assets of Europe in the balance. Even an antagonistic Europe not under Soviet sway or intimidation would be a distressing prospect to contemplate. Thus, diffusion of power suggests coalition diplomacy as the answer, at least in areas of deeply shared interest. The challenge of the 1980s will be to devise and perfect habits and procedures for coordination in responding to threats in new areas, of which the Middle East is the most compelling.

LIMITS OF A UNILATERAL US STRATEGY

Despite periodic excursions into consultation, the United States has generally acted alone. This is true not only in its pursuit of an Arab-Israeli peace, but also in its more recent efforts to bolster regional security. Frustrated by European attitudes, the United States has spent billions, with billions more planned, to create additional military assets; but these assets have applications other than in Southwest Asia.

Employing three separate military commands, the United States can claim an enhanced ability to project power into the region. The European Command (EUCOM) may be able to use military bases in Turkey—most yet to be built, and cooperation yet to be negotiated—to interdict Soviet approaches through Iran or Iraq. EUCOM, which also covers Israel, will continue trying to work out shared responsibilities for US avenues of approach from the west and for any other mission that Israel might be willing and politically acceptable to perform. Current thinking, considering the desirability of Arab cooperation, foresees no projection of Israeli strength eastward but, rather, a contribution in the Mediterranean.

The Pacific Command (PACOM) controls all assets in the Indian Ocean, up to the shores of the Arabian littoral. It is constructing, with British agreement, a huge main operating base on Diego Garcia. No country has been prepared to garrison American air and land forces on its soil; therefore, PACOM's carrier task forces provide the only real US combat presence in the region. Even Egypt—sympathetic and sophisticated regarding the political and military vulnerabilities of the Gulf—refused to permit the US Army battalion in Sinai to bring all organic equipment and support/transport needed for rapid deployment eastward.

Equipment for a Marine brigade (less aircraft) is deployed with ships off Diego Garcia. But the brigade's manning echelons would have to be flown to a location where they could join it. This would require the permission of one or more host governments in the Gulf region for landing both men and materiel. Because the Navy will not risk its carriers in the narrow confines of the Gulf, the Marines' forcible entry capability in the region is modest. Consequently, while amphibious lift for a battalion or two is available, air and naval artillery cover will be limited if operations are mounted anywhere but in the lower regions of the Gulf—far from the largest oil fields, which are at the northern end of the Gulf and closer to potential Soviet lines of advance.

Despite the "over the horizon" presence the Navy supplies—and over which the Navy jealously guards its control—PACOM is probably best suited to protection of sea lines of communications and early lodgment of US forces in distant locations like Oman and Bandar Abbas. Performance of even these missions would require local support and approval, but that approval might well be forthcoming. After all, a Soviet attack through Iran or Iraq not only will focus the minds of many local governments, but will probably be accompanied by attacks out of Afghanistan on the narrows of Hormuz and in the Indian Ocean.

This situation leaves the major task of projecting power in the region to the newly created Central Command (CENTCOM). CENTCOM can, as noted, probably count on some help from Marines landing in the lower Gulf. The main body of its force, however, must cross the Atlantic, Europe, the eastern Mediterranean, Egypt, and Saudi Arabia to deploy. Included would be both ground and air elements of the Marines, as well as larger contingents of Army and Air Force personnel. The numbers of men and aircraft that can be moved to the Gulf in a short time and sustained in combat over a long period are severely limited. They are much more limited if Turkey does not participate. And if the Saudis do not actively participate, US capability is questionable at best.

Deployment, not employment, therefore dictates the size of the force; the force is not sized to the Soviet threat. And the Soviets possess enormous advantages in nearby bases on Soviet soil and in Afghanistan. In fact, the Soviets seem clearly able to overwhelm an American force of almost any conceivable size in that theater, even assuming we could deploy with adequate warning—a critical and risky assumption.

Nevertheless, the size of the projected force is not the critical weakness of CENTCOM. Political weakness, not a military weakness at all, is most troubling. In the Middle East, unlike in Europe and Asia, we lack altogether the organizational structure and support facilities of an alliance. The region is, in fact, so divided against itself and us that alliances are impossible. Only certain varying kinds of cooperation are possible with Oman, Egypt, Jordan, Saudi Arabia, Pakistan, Israel, Somalia, and others. Division in the region has made for a highly adaptive and idiosyncratic strategy. Each initiative must be weighed against its impact on one or more other relationships. The absence of cooperation in one place vitiates cooperation elsewhere; the wrong kind of relationship in one case makes other relationships impossible. The entire CENTCOM mission depends on an invitation from—and advance coordination with—states that, so far, have not been prepared either to host US facilities or undertake advance coordination.

Therefore, the Reagan administration's shift in thinking was not strange: emphasis shifted from a reactive conflict at the point of invasion—with a rapidly deployable force large enough for the task—to a conflict that would spread quickly outside the region, at US initiative. Carter's policy was the opposite and dictated a large CENTCOM force. In making this shift, the administration did not reduce the requirements of the force, concerned as it is generally with force buildup; CENTCOM would ultimately be larger than as proposed by the Carter administration.[11] But the new policy made release of US forces to CENTCOM much less likely when escalation is planned elsewhere.

But where? This poses questions of a very different order—questions with direct impact on the Europeans. What target is comparable to the Middle East in importance to the Soviets? Not the Soviet fleet in the Indian and Pacific Oceans; not Cuba. The painful fact is that the West, Europe in particular, stands to be stopped in its tracks if oil ceases to flow from the Gulf. And no one has bothered to explain how, even with a successful blocking lodgment in the mountains of central Iran, we could seriously hope to prevent crippling blows against the fragile oil loading facilities in the Gulf. Indeed, the small and weak states of the region might in those circumstances worry that a US presence could produce, not deter, such attacks on oil loading facilities. One solution would be to make clear that attacks on Gulf oil facilities justify, in our view, counterattacks on comparable Soviet oil facilities. This would even out the oil stakes; but it would also set up an ominous scenario for homeland retaliation by the Soviets against us.

European cooperation can bolster the capacity of the West to respond rapidly and effectively to threats in Southwest Asia. Thus, it can offer both enhanced deterrence against Soviet threats and greater prospects for controlling escalation and confining a confrontation to that region, as well as terminating it short of more general hostilities. Such European cooperation seems to be even more in their interests than ours, considering their greater dependence on Middle East oil and, incidentally, their growing stake in Soviet energy supplies. We need an arrangement that goes considerably beyond the familiar conceptual framework of Atlantic security cooperation. The arrangement must encompass direct European military participation in the Middle East on a planned basis.

This participation could be alongside or through NATO. But wrenching the attention of EUCOM from the Fulda Gap is a daunting task; and there are, as some observers have noted, institutional difficulties in conceiving a confrontation with the USSR in the Gulf that would not inevitably affect Europe itself and involve NATO in any case. How could the United States engage Soviet forces in the Middle East without expecting a Warsaw Pact/NATO alert? This prospect may be distasteful for Western Europeans. But it is no less distasteful for Eastern Europeans who would have an interest in restraining a Soviet challenge, thereby adding to the deterrent impact of Western preparedness.

Establishing a formal security linkage between Europe and the Middle East might be wrenching to our allies. But NATO already holds exercises in the Caribbean; and the Gulf is, of course, north of the Tropic of Cancer and not much to the east of Turkey. So such a linkage is not unthinkable. Europeans must decide whether, in any case, hard choices would not be forced upon them by a faltering US defense effort in the Gulf. They must also consider whether perception of the United States as bearing alone the defense of important Western interests in the Middle East does not subvert the Alliance—both with Congress and the US public.

Moreover, the potential costs of creating such a linkage are at least partially offset by some advantages. A basis would be laid for multilateral—not just US—security assurances to major oil producers. European participation would not only enhance deterrence of the Soviets and go far toward assuring successful reaction to a Soviet adventure within the Middle East; it would also broaden the range of Western options in dealing with threats of lesser magnitude than Soviet invasion. It would permit the use of European assistance where appropriate without requiring direct superpower involvement. Finally, this reorientation would justify substantially greater aid to Turkey, an Ally that would become a pivot between Western defense of Europe and prevention of a Soviet drive through Iran and Iraq.

AGENDA FOR DIALOGUE

A serious new dialogue with Europe on the defense of Southwest Asia requires, in the first instance, an agenda and a venue. At least at the outset, the formal boundaries of NATO need not be expanded. Progress does require an agreed analysis of the danger to the Alliance's members and to the viability of its military posture from the major threats outlined above: (1) Soviet control or denial of oil; (2) internal instability, subversion, and local conflicts in the Middle East; and (3) a prolonged estrangement of drifting apart of Europe and the United States on questions of oil and Middle East policy.

The Harmel Exercise and Report provides a precedent for an exhaustive review by the Alliance. Oil disruption and the undeniable importance today of the Gulf certainly rival détente and French withdrawal from military participation as new and vital issues facing the Atlantic community. The threat analysis and broad strategic review might be undertaken for the Military Committee, postponing consideration of the vexing question of whether to extend NATO's operational boundaries or put other arrangements in place.[12]

Maybe the question of political boundaries can be sidestepped, perhaps by forming a new group, such as the High Level Group that dealt with certain nuclear questions. A Group on the Middle East could seat select countries on a regular basis, adding others in rotation or as desired. Alternatively, intensified consultation and planning outside the formal NATO structure, among Middle East and European experts of selected governments, may be preferable. The United States, Great Britain, France, Italy, and West Germany—whose military role would be, for constitutional reasons, within the NATO area (i.e., in Turkey)—appear to be the Alliance states with both substantial interests and capabilities to contribute. Such an extra-NATO arrangement would have an additional advantage. It would permit interaction and participation with other free world nations, such as Japan, Australia, and New Zealand. These nations have substantial interests in Gulf security, and they have naval, transport, and political capabilities to contribute.[13]

Whether established within or alongside the NATO structure, the new consultative and combined planning body's initial task would be to consider in detail the shared threat analysis and to recommend common action. Concerns of the security subcommittee would include the following:

- Declaratory policy, existing and recommended.
- Questions of force size and composition, including European contributions.
- Force presence in the Middle East.
- Bases, facilities, and other projection requirements.
- US-European contingency planning.
- Command arrangements and location.

- Combined exercise plans.

- Common acquisition programs, particularly for ships, aircraft, and air defense.

- Relative financial contributions and overall costs.

- Coordination mechanisms, political and military.

- Triggering events for deployment.

- Political objectives and liabilities of operations in the Middle East.

Consultation with Turkey on its role in a military contingency in Southwest Asia should receive special attention. Turkey's location would allow positioning of forces to menace the flanks and rear of a Soviet move southward through Azerbaijan. The defending force could then engage the Soviets well before they reach the Gulf littoral. An expansive system of secure bases in eastern Turkey would be required, and Turkey would become, in such a scenario, a NATO tripwire. At least limited NATO reinforcements, as well as heavy economic and military assistance to Turkey, would be needed in advance of a Soviet move. But recognition of Turkey's pivotal role could give the current NATO effort the focus it presently lacks. Clearly, this role could involve Turkey intricately in security missions in areas of the former Ottoman Empire as well as in Iran. But Turkey's oil supply is no less at risk than that of the rest of Europe.

Should the Allies seek to counter a Soviet move into the Gulf region so as to confine it geographically to that area or to expand it to other areas, including Europe? This is one of the most important and sensitive issues that NATO must confront. [14] Whether contemplating escalation or horizontal expansion, resolution of this issue is extremely difficult. Europeans must face the issue, however, because the answer largely determines force size and composition, specifically a European contribution. The United States at present has opted for a small force in the area. But it is developing a larger force—one it cannot sustain with its own resources and other commitments—as part of a deterrent strategy, which is part calculated bluff. The strategy will probably work; but it has the grave defect of requiring escalation outside the area, and it includes the possibility that the limited force could be overcome.

Reversion to the argument that perhaps Europe and the United States should not discuss these matters because they are too difficult is not an adequate response. The Americans might be tempted to accept that argument because the Europeans have failed to address these issues seriously thus far. After all, the effort to improve the coordination and effectiveness of a Western political and military strategy in the Gulf could deprive the United States of its relative freedom of action, so important to many elements in the American body politic. For Europeans, such a Western strategy could create controversy at home, problems in the Middle East, and increased costs, all to meet a threat that may not eventuate.

To argue that any effort to cope with the situation should be bilateral and ad hoc and should leave defense of the Gulf to unilateral US response is to take a head-in-the-sand approach. Such an approach is not likely to work. Both sides of the Atlantic must face the fact, palatable or not, that neither can succeed in the Middle East and minimize the risks without the other. US strategy, as now designed, will not work to protect European interests and leave them unaffected.

CONCLUSIONS AND RECOMMENDATIONS

At the present and for the foreseeable future, security of the region centering on the Persian Gulf undoubtedly will constitute a shared vital objective of the Atlantic community. The question for the United States and its Allies, whether or not it has been adequately aired, is not *whether* these interests will be defended, particularly against direct Soviet challenge, but *how*. How effectively and within what geographic and other limitations? In the face of a concrete Soviet military move, the Allies would likely cooperate. But the effectiveness of the effort—indeed, the capacity of Western readiness to deter a Soviet move—will be weakened, perhaps critically, by failure to plan and prepare a coordinated response *before* a crisis occurs.

How, then, do the Allies focus and channel their energies into the effort required? In large part, the absence of precedent complicates the problem. For the Allies, it is of a different order than the problem addressed by existing security arrangements, which commit the United States to come to the Allies' defense. For the United States, the challenge is *not* qualitatively different: to project military power into an area thousands of miles from home. The difference is that much of the on-the-ground infrastructure assumed in formal Alliance arrangements is nonexistent in the Gulf region. Therefore, the need increases for support from allies much nearer to the focus.

The unprecedented security threat we have discussed calls for imaginative and dramatic solutions. The problem does not fit neatly into any of the compartments—geographic, functional, or institutional—with which we and other Western governments have been accustomed to deal in the postwar world. It requires regular cooperation between our European and Middle East specialists and their counterparts from Europe.

We cannot define the Gulf area narrowly, separating the security problem there from political and security problems in the surrounding Middle East. Doing so flies in the face not only of logic and experience, but also of the objections of both local governments and Western partners. Nor can we equate potential US partners in such an effort with NATO alone. Some Allies will be reluctant to participate actively and, in any case, have little to contribute. Other nations not members of NATO have deep interests in the region and much to bring to bear.

If neither geographic, nor functional, nor institutional compartments will serve, neither will a purely military one if we are to attract and sustain the active cooperation of allies. Military preparedness is only one element, though not the least important, in avoiding military challenges to vital Western interests. Equally important, particularly in regions of chronic instability such as the Middle East, is the full range of political, diplomatic, economic, and security assistance relationships. We must be prepared to enter into a far more serious dialogue with the Allies on such problems as the Arab-Israeli conflict and its resolution. Otherwise, we are likely to gain neither the diplomatic support we deserve nor the security cooperation the Atlantic community needs.

Regular consultation on a full range of Middle East issues, including Gulf security, appears necessary. Within this framework, specifically military coordination can take place on premises that can be explained to European and other publics. So long as our global security policy is European-based, such consultation would be a normal part of any effort to provide leadership. Some measure of US capacity for independent action would be relinquished in the process, although it is easy to exaggerate the extent; it is difficult to conceive of any important US goal, including support for Israel's legitimate defense interests, that could be compromised in the process. And as already noted, the President's initiative of September 1982 provides a broadly acceptable basis for policy, so long as it is not permitted to languish as another example of US good intention and ineffective leadership.[15]

Effective Allied cooperation will require US initiative. Europe has demonstrated neither the will nor the imagination to provide such impetus. As a beginning, we recommend the establishment of regular consultations with selected European governments on a full range of Middle East political and security interests. These consultations should not draw on intelligence specialists, as do the semiannual NATO experts meetings. They should draw on officials at the Assistant Secretary level and below with operational responsibilities for both European and Middle East policy. The goal would be not just a frank exchange of views and proposals, but also personal familiarity and the development, over time, of a greater area of shared assumptions regarding both threats and opportunities.

Concurrently, existing NATO machinery could serve as a springboard, as outlined in the preceding section, to develop an agreed threat analysis for the Gulf region. With this in hand, a High Level Group comprising leading NATO members and other states, such as Japan, Australia, and New Zealand, should consider both the threat analysis and the resources each nation could contribute *if the Soviets moved into the Gulf region*.[16] The question of the relative likelihood of this threat need not stall the proceedings at this stage, as various scenarios are considered. Rigorous examination of US capabilities and strategy, along the lines we discussed earlier, should reveal serious deficiencies in the capacity of the West to meet a Soviet threat in the Gulf region. Non-US participants will also see that, as now planned, even a unilateral US defense effort there will inevitably affect Europe in a number of ways, including the probability of horizontal escalation. The Allies may not decide to undertake coordinated planning. But the debate will at least be shifted from US requests for assistance to contemplation of what the Allies can do with us to improve their own prospects and minimize risks.

At the outset at least, the most critical need would be not for significant Allied combat forces but for commitment of facilities and resources to support the US deployment. In a major operation, substantial combined operations in a Gulf theater might even have serious operational drawbacks. But this is a question for later consideration. The task now is to focus attention and push measures with short term payoffs. In the Appendix, we have included a list of marginal measures the Allies can take immediately to enhance the capability of the US deployment. Some, such as transit and basing facilitation, are clearly of a greater magnitude than others. But each would be important in developing the sense of shared burden and stake the situation demands.

In the short run, even minor Allied troop contributions to a putative deployment force would likely yield important advantages. The designation of elected units would send a signal to the Soviets and others that would, in itself, have a deterrent effect. Beyond that, however, one can imagine situations in which limited forces from European states might be more acceptable locally and less disruptive globally than the dispatch of US troops, with all its implications for superpower rivalry. Given the sensitivities of both Europeans and others, this is not a minor consideration. We may be seeing some manifestations of increased European awareness of this fact. French, Italian, and British contributions to the multilateral force in Lebanon and European contingents in the Sinai Multinational Force constitute highly responsible contributions. These contributions stand out all the more in the general absence of serious consideration of the potential demands of Gulf security.

Ultimately, only our European and other allies can decide whether they have the will and capability to participate effectively in the defense of their own interests. The process we have recommended the United States put in motion provides the opportunity for placing the decision squarely before them. If they see and accept the challenge—not on our behalf, but for themselves—we will have gone far toward restoring Allied consensus and focusing it on a new and vital area of challenge. From that consensus, new institutions, such as a combined command for the Gulf, could follow. But as we made woefully clear at the outset, we are far from such a point in terms of political consultations and public acceptance. If, despite our best and most sincere efforts, the Allies choose to ignore or fail to discern the need for shared effort, they cannot but accept the right of the United States to pursue its interests by whatever means remain.

APPENDIX
AGENDA FOR SHORT-TERM ENHANCEMENT

European partners could quickly develop a number of measures, simply to buttress US efforts, without immediately involving Europe deeply in new commitments:

Access/en route basing/overflight rights. Of all the problems CENTCOM has in planning a deployment, none is so complex and uncertain as the routes for deployment. Bilateral air agreements exist with Britain, France, Germany, Portugal, Italy, Spain, Greece, and Turkey—all NATO countries—but no combined agreement exists. In the bilaterals, each country has the prerogative to deny access or overflight, and for exercises in the region, access has been denied. A maximum of 300 sorties per day could transit NATO countries. If an agreement could be worked out so the United States knew for sure how the airflow would go, it would enhance planning. As it is, assumptions are made that may not be corrected, and bottlenecks due to available ramp space or fuel might result.

Strategic/tactical airlift support. All the Allies have airlift assets, which have been made more important by the absence of basing in Southwest Asia.

Sealift. The European Allies have double the merchant ships that are available to the United States. The NATO pool contains over 400 dry-cargo ships, and Japan has considerable assets. These ships are vital to the supply line to either Southwest Asia or NATO regions. The United States should negotiate an agreement with NATO for the availability of these ships. US shipping is spread around the world at any one time, and only a portion would be available on short notice.

Sea lines of communication (SLOC) security. The 600-ship US Navy is not a reality—even if it was, it probably could not protect the SLOC to Southwest Asia. The distance is 13,000 miles and the threat from the Soviet submarine fleet is large. The NATO fleets could assist in this endeavor.

Air lines of communication (ALOC) security. The primary air route to Southwest Asia goes through the Mediterranean. Both Libya and Syria could pose potential threats to the ALOC. Positioning aircraft carriers en route precludes their use in Southwest Asia. Both the Italians and French could provide support if Libya became involved.

Unit support. The United States is short in combat support/combat service support units for Southwest Asia (e.g., engineer, port handling, intelligence, and air defense units). If the Allies could designate or form special units in these areas, training and planning could be coordinated. Both France and Britain have special operations type forces that could assist the United States. Both have past colonial ties to the region, providing experience and intelligence assets in some areas that could be invaluable.

Medical support. Critical shortages exist both in capability and in treatment facilities. Almost all Allies could assist in this area.

Antimine/mine warfare. The United States has four minesweepers in the regular Navy and 52 in the reserve fleet. None are in Southwest Asia, and it would take them much too long to arrive on the scene after mobilization to be effective. The French had a squadron of minesweepers in Djibouti; the NATO Allies have several hundred in NATO waters. Rotation of a squadron of minesweepers from NATO countries to the area, the sharing of deep-sea antimine warfare with the Allies, and joint research and development in this field could make important contributions. The US Navy has three mine countermeasures helicopter squadrons, but they are not in Southwest Asia and require extensive airlift to deploy.

Security assistance. This effort requires coordination. Rather than each country trying to sell weapon systems in every country in Southwest Asia, a coordinated plan should be presented to the regional countries that will enhance their regional security framework. For example, there are several air defense systems in the region, but in the absence of interoperability, they cannot be combined to contribute to regional defense. If one country sold air defense, another tactical aircraft, another land weapons, it might standardize systems and contribute to a framework for regional security.

Linguists. It takes several years to train Arabic or Farsi linguists, not to mention the problem of incentives to maintain fluency. A study in the Office of the Secretary of Defense, Manpower, Reserve Affairs, and Logistics (OSD, MRA&L), is under consideration to decide the best course. But in the meantime, the deficiency might be filled by linguists from Britain, France, and perhaps Italy.

Contingency planning. If we succeed in sharing the burden of Gulf security with NATO Allies, then the next logical step would be to involve them in planning for the area. As mentioned in the strategy, US response is threat oriented. Going one step beyond planning, NATO Allies could respond instead of the United States. European Allies could handle a number of lower magnitude threats by deploying their own units to the region. A combined strategy could be developed for regional areas within Southwest Asia and for response to requests from specific countries, such as France–Horn of Africa, Britian–Persian Gulf Littoral, United States–Saudi Arabia. All should understand that US support may be required for airlift or logistics; but shared responsibility would improve the regional countries' perception of the United States and could avoid superpower confrontation in the area.

5

AUSTRALIA, AMERICA, AND INDIAN OCEAN SECURITY:
POSSIBILITIES FOR INCREASED COOPERATION

by

Kevin J. McGuire
Department of State

Thomas D. Pilsch
Colonel, US Air Force

John W. Stark
Captain, US Navy

Kevin J. McGuire, US Department of State, specializes in economic affairs and has served in Canberra and Adelaide, Australia. Colonel Thomas D. Pilsch, US Air Force, has a broad background in global military airlift operations and logistics. Captain John W. Stark, US Navy, has extensive experience in the Pacific and Indian Ocean theaters. All three authors are 1983 graduates of the National War College.

INTRODUCTION

In recent years, events in Southwest Asia, particularly the Persian Gulf, have preoccupied US foreign policy planners. The Soviet Navy's increasing presence in the Indian Ocean and the Soviet Army's southward thrust into Afghanistan sharply heightened American interest in the region. In response, the United States increased its naval presence in the Indian Ocean and created a new unified command, the US Central Command (CENTCOM).

These initiatives revealed glaring deficiencies in US regional resources. Success of our policies clearly depends on the level of cooperation we can achieve with regional friends, specifically those in the Indian Ocean littoral.

Australia has critical economic and security interests in the Indian Ocean. It shares with us a time-tested alliance, a compatible world view, and similar economic, political, and social aspirations. US security policy in the Indian Ocean requires an investment of military resources and diplomatic initiatives that exceeds the scope of this paper. Clearly, however, greater Australian-American cooperation would contribute substantially to a more coordinated, cost-effective, and forward-looking policy than now exists.

This essay examines possibilities for increasing bilateral cooperation in defense of the Indian Ocean and makes specific recommendations for action. The recommendations are tempered by the knowledge of facts that severely limit the range and scope of possible shared activity: Australia's modest defense budget, its distance from current hot spots, and the expected policies of the newly elected Australian Labor Party (ALP) government. Some suggestions are simple, such as ways to improve policy consultation. Others seem obvious but have long been neglected, such as joint planning, especially in those areas where Australia is expected to make a critical contribution in a crisis or war situation.

Of potentially greater significance and longer term value are those suggestions that deal with improving Australia's sea control capability and support infrastructure while avoiding offense to Australian sensibilities on foreign basing. These include possible US contributions to the development of Australian naval and air facilities in Western Australia and assistance in the Australian acquisition of an aircraft carrier. Other proposals would promote regional coproduction of defense items to encourage more efficient procurement and promote a higher degree of allied interoperability. Finally, there are those proposals that, to be accepted, will require considerable and persistent effort, such as convincing Australia to carry a larger share of the regional defense burden.

The United States already enjoys a high level of cooperation with Australia in defense matters. But the authors feel efforts should proceed to improve and expand our joint capability to defend free world interests in the Indian Ocean. The United States should, however, be careful not to provoke a reaction from the ALP government that would jeopardize current arrangements. The authors recommend a careful approach, designed to protect the status of joint-use installations available to us in Australia. Such a strategy would start with simple, noncontroversial proposals and progress toward those with greater, longer lasting benefit to both countries. Eventually, the United States could broach those proposals that carry a higher price tag for Australia but contribute to allied military strength in the region.

THE INDIAN OCEAN AS A STRATEGIC CROSSROAD

In the aftermath of the Iranian revolution and the Soviet occupation of Afghanistan, the Indian Ocean and its littoral has risen among US defense priorities. The problem of deploying and supporting forces in this vast, remote region has demonstrated the limitations in US defense resources and has prompted efforts to improve our capability in the Indian Ocean. One avenue to enhanced regional capability is cooperation with other nations in the area. This essay specifically examines the possibility of greater Australian-American cooperation in the defense of mutual Indian Ocean interests.

Problems in the Indian Ocean

A variety of factors have combined in recent years to focus international attention on the Indian Ocean, the Persian Gulf, and Southwest Asia. The southward thrust of Soviet naval and land forces is among the most significant of these factors. The Soviet buildup of naval presence in the region since the mid-1960s prompted a countervailing US effort and the development of Diego Garcia as a regional base. But events in Iran and Afghanistan in 1979 are what sharply focused US concern on the potential consequences of the loss of Western access to Middle Eastern oil and on the Soviet Union's emergence as a preeminent power in the region. The prospect of Soviet control of vital petroleum resources and sea lines of communication (SLOC) signaled the need for a strengthened free world posture to protect our own and allied interests. Unless we greatly change our relations with Moscow or reassess our interests, our commitment to this region will remain strong.

Strategists are naturally concerned that US resources to defend the region are limited. We lack support facilities in the area, and our naval forces are already so heavily committed in other theaters that a permanent presence strains existing resources. Reacting to this shortage of naval resources, the US Navy developed and is employing a flexible operations (FLEXOPS) policy. This policy enables the Navy to meet standing commitments for carrier battle groups (CVBGs) in the Mediterranean and western Pacific while maintaining the ability to respond to a crisis in the Indian Ocean on short notice. As a result of FLEXOPS, the Navy was able to maintain two CVBGs in the Indian Ocean in 1979 at the height of the Iranian crisis.

The creation of the Rapid Deployment Joint Task Force (RDJTF) and US Central Command [1] further reflects US commitment. It also makes additional demands on available manpower and materiel. Obviously, efficient use of our scarce defense resources and those of our allies requires maximum cooperation. The present lack of regional infrastructure to support extended operations by US forces is a major problem. And we have little prospect for dramatic improvement in the near future. While our main Indian Ocean base, Diego Garcia, is extremely useful, its small size and remoteness limit its potential. Clearly, establishment of an adequate regional support infrastructure through cooperation with friendly nations on the Indian Ocean littoral would contribute significantly to sustaining major US operations and to discouraging Soviet aggression.

Despite modest progress in gaining cooperation with Indian Ocean littoral nations, glaring deficiencies in our capabilities persist. Some littoral states vocally support an American regional presence but do not wish bases or significant support facilities on their soil. Others lack useful facilities, the economic sophistication to render meaningful support, or strategic position. Many wish to avoid any involvement in what they see as a superpower conflict. Still others are aligned with the USSR. The long term political stability of some regional nations is questionable; this poses a serious impediment to any major US investment in military facilities. In addition, responsible US officials are reluctant, given budget realities, to suggest duplicating in the Indian Ocean facilities that already exist in the Philippines and other western Pacific bases.

US Goals in the Indian Ocean

Faced with this imperfect situation relative to force projection and support facilities, the United States should consider all possible ways to counter Soviet influence and military capability in the region. Possibilities include—

- improving combat and surveillance capabilities to support sea control and SLOC protection missions;

- encouraging allied awareness of and involvement in Indian Ocean and Southwest Asian defense;

- improving the cost-effectiveness of the US presence in this region; and

- hedging against the loss of existing military facilities because of hostilities or other factors.

In acting to achieve these goals, the United States must bear in mind fiscal realities (both American and allied), the acceptability of possible options to the American public, popular sentiment in any country choosing to cooperate with us, and world opinion.

The authors contend that in pursuing the above objectives the United States has neglected opportunities for securing assistance from Australia—the Indian Ocean littoral nation most likely to share our perceptions on regional issues, already a security alliance (ANZUS) partner, and a friend of long standing.

PROSPECTS FOR AUSTRALIAN-AMERICAN COOPERATION

Australia offers possibilities for further Indian Ocean cooperation. But this is not to suggest that Australia offers solutions to all of the problems confronting the United States in that region. Australia is located far from the current Southwest Asian hot spots, possesses a small population and modest military power, and is currently in an economic recession. Still, Australia offers some unique possibilities as a military support base and a regional political and military actor.

Australia as an Indian Ocean Power

Location. Despite its distance from the Persian Gulf, Western Australia is as close to it and to Diego Garcia, in terms of steaming days, as is Subic Bay in the Philippines. And sea transit from Western Australia to the northern Indian Ocean avoids the Indonesian straits. Increased Soviet presence in South Asia, particularly at Cam Ranh Bay, could make these chokepoints dangerous or impassable in time of crisis. A closure of these straits might mean a heavy US military reliance on Australian support facilities in a protracted conflict.

Regional actor. Australia is an Indian Ocean littoral state and has specially emphasized maintaining good relationships with such strategically located neighbors as Indonesia, Malaysia, and Singapore. Australia plays a positive political role because of its status as a littoral state. One example of this is its important moderating influence since 1976 on proposals for an Indian Ocean Zone of Peace.

Australian interests in the Indian Ocean. Australians have traditionally regarded themselves as members of the Pacific Community, and their defense policy has consistently reflected this self-perception. However, over the past 20 years, Australians have increasingly come to recognize their self-interest in a secure Indian Ocean as well. The new prominence of Western Australia, with its immense mineral resources, has sensitized Australia to the importance of an Indian Ocean dimension to its defense efforts. Western Australia is no longer excluded from national defense strategy. Australian exports to Japan—largely minerals from Western Australia—account for 30 percent of total exports and 10 percent of Australian gross domestic product (GDP).

Australia's connection to the Middle East also figures prominently in this new awareness of the Indian Ocean. Middle Eastern oil accounts for 30 percent of Australian petroleum requirements.[2] Exports to the Middle East reached 1.1 billion Australian dollars ($A) in 1982 (6 percent of total exports), and sales from the important agricultural sector were especially strong.[3]

Fifty percent of Australia's trade, by tonnage, now passes through the Indian Ocean. The Suez Canal provides a key link for Australian-European trade. The canal, the Indonesian straits, and the Indian Ocean SLOC also have an important indirect effect on the Australian economy: each is essential to the economic well-being of Japan, Australia's biggest customer and trading partner. Clearly, Australia has a major stake in the security of the Indian Ocean.

A common commitment to a secure Indian Ocean. Australia has cooperated with the United States in numerous ways to enhance the defense capabilities of the free world. The limited scope of this essay precludes an extensive review of Australian-American cooperation to date. But Australian participation in the Korean and Vietnam Wars and in the Sinai Multinational Force illustrates the depth of this cooperation and commitment. So does the hosting of critical joint Australian-American communications and defense monitoring establishments at North West Cape, Alice Springs, and Nurringar.[4]

The ANZUS Treaty has served as the keystone for Australian defense and foreign policy since its signing in 1952 by Australia, New Zealand, and the United States. The text of the ANZUS Treaty focuses on the Pacific and is not explicit with regard to Indian Ocean responsibilities.[5] None of the three partners has sought clarification of the treaty's applicability to this area. At some future time, confronting this question directly may prove necessary or desirable. But it serves no useful purpose to do so now.

For the present, the real issue is not legalistic. It is whether and to what extent the Australian and American governments wish to collaborate in Indian Ocean security. In the late 1970s, before the Soviet invasion of Afghanistan, Australian Prime Minister Malcolm Fraser risked becoming *persona non grata* in Washington by his frequent admonitions about the need for increased strength in the Indian Ocean. Fraser was most concerned about President Carter's decision to work toward a bilateral agreement with the Soviet Union limiting Indian Ocean naval strength—a decision that was not discussed with Australia before it was announced.[6] Events in Afghanistan in late 1979 converted the Carter administration to Fraser's view.

The Australian government has since assisted in strengthening allied Indian Ocean presence in a number of ways, including the following:

- Royal Australian Navy (RAN) vessel participation in northwestern Indian Ocean patrols (the RAN flagship, the carrier HMAS *Melbourne*, among them).

- Invitations for frequent US Navy ship visits to Australian ports (43 in 1982).

- Permission for the staging of US Air Force B–52 surveillance and training flights from Australian airfields.

- Hosting of joint land/sea/air exercises in Western Australia.

- Progress on new naval facilities at HMAS Stirling (south of Perth at Cockburn Sound), which is scheduled to support a new, permanent Indian Ocean presence of four RAN escorts and two submarines.

In 1980, Prime Minister Fraser invited the United States to establish a home port for a carrier battle group (CVBG) at Cockburn Sound. The invitation has neither been accepted nor rejected by the United States. But it at least reconfirmed Australia's commitment to a joint approach to Indian Ocean security matters.

A stable, democratic friend with shared aspirations. Australia is one of the few nations on the Indian Ocean littoral, or indeed in the world, that enjoys stability, democracy, and a genuinely free society. In addition, Australians share with Americans a unique frontier experience; this has contributed to the formation of cultures with many common attitudes and aspirations. Experience shows that Australia and the United States are as likely as any two nations in the world to agree and cooperate on challenges to fundamental political rights and economic well-being.

Australians have a highly positive opinion of the United States, which extends to their view of the ANZUS Alliance. For example, a nationwide poll published by *The Melbourne Age* on 25 October 1982 revealed that 58 percent of those polled approved of visits by US naval ships, even when carrying nuclear weapons; and this matter has been one of the most controversial in our relationship. Variation from state to state in the level of support for such visits was slight, except that, notably, in Western Australia 65 percent favored them. In August 1981, the national newspaper, *The Australian,* reported that the Northern Territory's chief minister had suggested that Darwin become a base for US warships. This does not mean that Australians accept the American security connection without reservation or qualification, as Desmond Ball's critical book, *A Suitable Piece of Real Estate,* demonstrates. But by and large, Australians like Americans and have a positive image of the alliance's importance to their security.

Party Politics and Defense Policy in Australia

Significant differences exist among the major political parties' approaches to national security. At the risk of oversimplification, the Liberal Party (LP) and the National Country Party (NCP) have tended to be more concerned about the worldwide threat of communist aggression; more inclined toward a forward defense policy; and more eager to establish ways to strengthen the alliance with America and contribute to common efforts to contain communism. In short, ANZUS and the American connection have been close to, if not at the heart of, the LP/NCP approach to national security questions.

The Australian Labor Party (ALP), on the other hand, tends to favor a more "fortress Australia" approach; show less enthusiasm for actively cooperating with the United States on defense; and give a more sympathetic hearing to Third World views (for example, on the Indian Ocean Zone of Peace issue), even when this means a clash with US policy. However, this is not to suggest that the ALP's view of what is good for Australia is based on an anti-US attitude or that ALP perceptions are necessarily antithetical to those of the United States.

The ALP has been in power only 3 years in recent decades. But on 5 March 1983, it won a resounding victory over the LP/NCP coalition, which has dominated the post-World War II political scene. The economy and the popularity of the two primary candidates overshadowed all other issues in the campaign. So the ALP election does not appear to reflect a significant change in Australian attitudes on defense matters.[7]

Australian-American relations will remain warm regardless of the party in office. From the point of view of increased Indian Ocean collaboration with the United States, however, an LP/NCP government would almost certainly have been a more enthusiastic partner than the ALP.

Exactly what line new Prime Minister Robert Hawke will follow remains to be seen. Although long prominent as a labor leader, he was selected party head just before the campaign and has served only one term in Parliament. By past performance, he is bright, is favorably disposed toward the United States and a close bilateral security relationship, and should prove a strong leader. The new government, in the brief period since its formation, has clearly indicated that it regards ANZUS as fundamentally important; that it plans no basic changes in the current bilateral security relationship; and specifically, that joint facilities, ship visits, and B–52 flights will be continued.

Australian Defense Forces

Australia is one of the strongest military powers in the Indian Ocean littoral. Still, its small population and modest economic base sharply limit its power. Active military personnel barely number 73,000.[8] In 1979, the Fraser government promised a 5-year defense improvement program reflecting an annual 7 percent real growth in defense expenditures. Unfortunately, unfavorable economic conditions have delayed fulfillment of that promise. But we can expect the new government to continue some buildup.

Australia is in the process of major equipment acquisitions that will determine the direction of its defense capabilities into the 21st century.[9] The largest of these—in fact, the largest single defense purchase in Australian history—involves the acquisition of 75 F/A-18 fighter-bombers at a cost of $A2.4 billion.[10] These aircraft will offer a much greater capability than the aging Mirage III fighters they will replace.

Australia's frustrating effort to acquire an aircraft carrier to replace HMAS *Melbourne* has more immediate impact on Australian-American defense efforts in the Indian Ocean. Canberra had concluded an agreement in early 1982 to purchase HMS *Invincible* from the Royal Navy. Although *Invincible* was not its first choice of contending designs, Australia could not pass up the timing and cost of the purchase.[11] Following the success of *Invincible* in the Falkland Islands, the British government decided to withdraw its offer and refund the Australian deposit. This decision has left the RAN without a replacement for *Melbourne* and Australia with a major gap in its maritime defenses.[12] The decision also reopened the debate on the need for an aircraft carrier.[13] But the election of an ALP government has, at least for the immediate future, laid to rest any prospects for purchasing a carrier.

The RAN is purchasing four *Oliver Hazard Perry* (FFG-7)-class frigates from the United States, to be delivered between 1981 and 1984. Australia also is planning to construct as many as six more of these ships in domestic shipyards.[14]

Finally, Australia has decided to replace 10 older Royal Australian Air Force (RAAF) P-3B Orion long range maritime patrol (LRMP) aircraft with the newer, more capable P-3C version of the Orion. This will maintain at 20 the number of LRMP aircraft in the RAAF inventory. These aircraft are ideal resources for patrolling and controlling the vast sea approaches to Australia, the key straits to the north, and the vital SLOC into the Indian and Pacific Oceans. Unfortunately, the lack of sufficient aircrews seriously degrades the potential effectiveness of the RAAF Orion force. The present ratio of .7 crews per aircraft has been a source of controversy and offers a ready target for the improvement of Australian maritime capabilities.[15]

Neither the government nor the political parties have defined an unambiguous defense strategy for the late 1980s or 1990s. The partisan nature of national security policy inhibits the production of such a plan.

Minister of Defense Ian Sinclair, in a November 1982 speech to the Australian Defense Association, identified a perhaps even more relevant factor: "The problems of planning for Australia's defense are made more complex because we are not confronted with an immediate, easily identifiable threat to our national security." The Australian Parliament's Committee on Foreign Affairs and Defense reached the same conclusion in 1981.[16]

Lack of an explicit long term military strategy has not prevented Australians from maintaining an active interest in regional stability and assuming a broad (i.e., Western oriented) view of Australia's security interests. The decision to purchase an aircraft carrier (although now reversed) and the F/A-18, coupled with increased P-3 operations from Butterworth airfield in Malaysia and a buildup of new naval facilities in the north and west, reflect growing concern for Australia's medium to long term defense needs. These and other signs indicate that a systematic long term strategy for Australian defense may be on the way.

SUGGESTIONS FOR GREATER COOPERATION

The following are specific measures that the United States might usefully pursue to increase cooperation with Australia in the Indian Ocean. Some are simple and immediately applicable while others may become more practical and attractive with time.

Bilateral Consultations and Coordination

The Australians are sensitive to being consulted (or at least being kept informed) about developments in US policy on matters of common interest. This is a natural concern of a loyal and supportive friend who has occasionally been embarrassed by unannounced zigzags in US positions (for example, on relations with China in the early 1970s and on Indian Ocean naval limitation). Historically, the problem lies at the highest levels of the US government and is, therefore, difficult to resolve. It results from carelessness and a lack of sensitivity rather than from a deliberate attempt to mislead.

In the future, the United States must guard against taking the Australians for granted. While we have a generally good record on exchanging information in the defense area, we can do more. The recent decision to conduct frequent ANZUS "officials talks" should usefully reinforce annual ministerial and other consultations. These meetings provide an excellent forum for in-depth exchanges on strategically important areas, perhaps including the Indian Ocean.

To foster a coordinated defense posture for the Indian Ocean, one or more Australian officers should be attached to the new US Central Command (CENTCOM). These officers must be of sufficient rank to ensure that Canberra regards their reports seriously and to ensure access to senior US officers. Increased liaison through a similar arrangement with the US Pacific Command (PACOM) will continue to be an important factor in Australian defense planning.

The suggestions above are hardly dramatic. A more significant departure from current practice would be to initiate joint Australian-American defense planning. Planning for the defense of the straits separating the Indian and Pacific Oceans would be a first, limited step. These straits are of critical importance in wartime and are an area where the Australians can play a key defense role. The Collins-Radford agreement of 1951 recognizes this. It assigns to the Australians general responsibility for wartime security of the Indian Ocean approaches to these straits.

Any initiative on joint planning should be at the level of the Secretary of Defense and his Australian counterpart. Such discussions should address planning for only the eastern Indian Ocean. The prospect for broader regional planning should be favorable if the initial efforts prove mutually acceptable. Throughout such a process, US participants must assure that the plans result from a partnership effort and fully reflect Australian interests.

Such planning could also take place within ANZUS, but significant institutional changes would be required. ANZUS reform goes beyond the scope of this essay, and as indicated above, ANZUS responsibilities in the Indian Ocean are not clearly defined. Nevertheless, more structured ANZUS relationships clearly can alleviate the types of problems addressed in this section. Establishment of an ANZUS secretariat is not a new idea, but its implementation may be overdue. It would be an ideal step toward greater information exchange, better coordination, and more cost-effective operations.[17]

As Australia begins to develop a long term defense strategy, the frank and full exchange of views is in the best interests of both nations. The specific US role should be to assist the Australians by making clear our own plans and capabilities for the Indian Ocean and sharing thoughts on how to combine efforts to our common advantage.

Use of HMAS Stirling and the Cockburn Sound Complex [18]

Cockburn Sound lies south of Perth on the western coast of Australia. Two port facilities are located there: Fremantle to the north and HMAS Stirling to the south. HMAS Stirling was commissioned in 1978. It presently has the capacity to support up to four ships of destroyer/frigate size and up to three submarines. The master plan for the base, however, provides for about four times that capacity, to include a large ship pier (approximately 1,500 feet in length) and a 630-foot extension to the destroyer wharf. With these additions, HMAS Stirling's facilities would be adequate to berth a US carrier battle group. The existing maintenance facilities are extensive and offer a wide variety of repair services. Electrical power, water, and sewage treatment facilities present no problems for expanded use. External utility hookups for vessels are available at existing wharfs but would have to be expanded in capacity to accommodate more ships. The Perth/Fremantle area has no drydocks of suitable capacity. The closest drydock capable of handling a destroyer or frigate is at Melbourne; a larger drydock is located at Brisbane.

Marine diesel fuel supplies are adequate at both the Fremantle port facility and at HMAS Stirling for routine port visit purposes. But reserve tankage and berthing space for fueling are limited. Either Fremantle or Stirling would need a substantial increase in tank capacity to support a US carrier battle group. Jet fuel (JP–5) is not routinely stocked to provide for carrier resupply. Negotiations on fuel exchange agreements and logistic resupply requirements are presently underway in Navy-to-Navy talks. Mutual agreement on fuel tankage and facility access would be helpful if current usage is maintained; it is critical to expanded use of the Cockburn Sound complex by the US Navy.

No aircraft support facility is included as part of the Cockburn Sound complex. The closest suitable facilities are at Perth International Airport, 11 miles northwest of Perth, and at RAAF Pearce, 17 miles north of Perth. Both airports are suitable for occasional use by US Navy aircraft. However, each would need expanded parking area, fuel storage, and maintenance hangers if a carrier were to use HMAS Stirling regularly.

Facilities at the Cockburn Sound complex are modest compared to those at the US Navy's main western Pacific operating base at Subic Bay in the Philippines. The depth and range of repair facilities, together with an adjacent naval air station at Cubi Point, make the Subic Bay complex uniquely capable of supporting Pacific Fleet operations.

However, expanded use of Cockburn Sound offers two advantages. First, although only marginally closer than Subic Bay to Diego Garcia, Cockburn Sound offers passage to the Indian Ocean unconstrained by straits or chokepoints. Right of passage is often taken for granted, but the ability to use these straits may be severely tested in the future. As the recent Law of the Sea negotiations highlighted, the right of passage, especially by military vessels, through the Indonesian straits is subject to question so long as the United States is not a signatory to the Law of the Sea Convention.[19] Furthermore, passage through these straits in time of war could be denied by blockage or mining. Prudence dictates that the United States encourage the development of an Indian Ocean support base as an alternative to Subic Bay. Cockburn Sound presents just such an alternative.

The second reason to expand use of Cockburn Sound is to improve the US bargaining position with the Philippine government for continued use of Subic Bay. In 1947, the United States established the right to exclusive use—rent free—of Subic Bay (reaffirmed through a mutual defense treaty in 1951). Since then, that right has eroded. Most recently, the 1979 amendments to the 1947 Philippine-US basing agreement granted continued use of the Philippine bases in return for a 5-year package of $500 million in security assistance. This is still a bargain by any standards. However, implicit in the agreement was a pledge of $80 million per year in economic development. Additionally, and perhaps more significantly because of long term implications, the 1979 amendment reduced the acreage retained as US facilities, acknowledged Philippine sovereignty over the bases, and provided for thorough reviews of the basing agreements at 5-year intervals.[20]

No one is suggesting that the United States abandon Subic Bay. However, President Marcos has stated publicly that the US bases in the Philippines eventually will be phased out.[21] Future negotiations will probably yield more constraints and require a higher price for use of these facilities. Increasing difficulties with access to Philippine bases would be even more probable should a new administration, less favorably disposed to the United States than the present Marcos regime, come to power.

The United States can take advantage of the facilities at Cockburn Sound in several specific ways:

US carrier home-porting. In 1980, the Australian government offered to discuss the home-porting of a US carrier at Cockburn Sound.[22] The next year, a US Navy technical team evaluated the small naval facility. The team found the cost to develop the base as a carrier home port would be excessive. This was especially true because the US Navy's drive to build a 600-ship fleet placed heavy demands on its portion of the US defense budget. Furthermore, in the broader context of whether or not home-porting a second carrier abroad (USS *Midway* is based in Japan) would substantially improve the Navy's ability to perform its mission, other sites were perhaps better suited from a strategic standpoint than Cockburn Sound.[23]

The US Navy is continuing to weigh its options for home-porting a second carrier abroad. Under present conditions and in view of competing priorities for Navy funds (primarily the 600-ship Navy), approval of such a plan is not likely.[24] However, developments in the Indian Ocean or Persian Gulf might warrant our increased and sustained presence in the region; and right of passage through the Indonesian straits might become a problem due to a disagreement with that country over the Law of the Sea Treaty. Either of these occurrences would cast the home-porting of a carrier at HMAS Stirling in a more favorable light. Thus, helping Australia build and maintain the necessary support infrastructure at Cockburn Sound is in the United States' best interest. It should keep this home-porting option open for future consideration.

Scheduled repair and upkeep of US Navy ships. One obvious measure to assist in the development of the Cockburn Sound complex would be the use of these facilities by the US Navy for scheduled maintenance during assigned in-port periods. A portion of the repair and upkeep of Seventh Fleet ships presently performed at Subic Bay and Singapore could be assigned to HMAS Stirling. This activity would promote the growth of Cockburn Sound beyond what would be realized through Australian resources alone.

Beside building an infrastructure to support our future needs, US use of this complex would—

- help underwrite the cost of assigning RAN escort ships to Western Australia, thus assisting Australia as it orients its defenses toward the Indian Ocean.

- have a salutary effect on Australian-American relations by contributing to the Western Australian economy.

- provide some leverage in negotiating basing agreements with the Philippines.

- provide a needed alternative in case of right-of-passage disputes with Indonesia.

US Presence in Western Australia

Development of Western Australia as a prime source of raw materials and as a base for unconstrained access to the Indian Ocean elevates its importance to the military planner. In recognition of Western Australia's role in an Indian Ocean strategy, the United States has increased activity in this region in the last decade. This level of activity must at least be sustained; where possible it should be expanded.

Joint exercises. Western Australia affords the military planner unlimited stretches of beach to practice amphibious landings of the type anticipated in the Indian Ocean. Indeed, the very fact of such exercises in the region has political significance. US participants in the Sandgroper and Kangaroo series of exercises lauded these opportunities for mutually beneficial training. The US Marine Corps is particularly keen to participate in exercises in this area.[25]

Worthwhile as these exercises might be, they seem to lack an objective. Fundamental to the application of military forces in defense of a region is a set of plans based on mutually negotiated responses to contingencies. Such planning would require that the United States provide Australia with an insight into the type and extent of commitment to defense of the region based on various scenarios. For example, assisting sea control and SLOC protection in the eastern reaches of the Indian Ocean and Indonesian archipelago are obvious missions for the RAN and the US Navy in time of war. Future exercises should test Australian ability to provide forces to carry out these tasks along with the joint tactics and functions of Australian-American interoperability. As far as can be determined, no plans exist for contingencies in the Indian Ocean such as exist in the NATO arena. Perhaps our common language misleads us into thinking that our navies can meet at sea and work out such problems as we go. Obviously, to enhance our mutual defensive posture, we should base our exercises with Australian forces on predetermined agreements on forces assigned, areas of responsibility, and approved/standardized tactical doctrine.[26]

Increased ship visits. Nothing demonstrates American presence as visibly or as favorably as visits by US ships. Frequent ship visits will exercise access privileges to Western Australia while demonstrating our ability and resolve to project power and promote regional stability in the Indian Ocean. Concurrently, ship visits contribute to the development of Western Australia by increasing use of port facilities and infusing money into local economies. The economic and public relations impact of such visits is greatest on smaller ports. Despite recent, well publicized controversy surrounding visits of US nuclear-powered vessels to ports in some Australian states, the Fraser government made it clear that it welcomed visits by all US ships. Apparently, the new ALP government will also welcome these visits. Ship visits are undoubtedly a low-risk, low-expense means of cementing Australian-American relations at their roots.

Base for US maritime prepositioning. Albany Bay, at the southwestern tip of Australia, was a staging point during World War II for convoys between Australia and Great Britain. It offers a well protected harbor with sufficient depth and anchorages for the US Navy maritime prepositioning ships to be used in the Indian Ocean. The advantage of a safe, assured location with unimpeded access to the Indian Ocean offsets the disadvantage of its distance from the Persian Gulf.[27]

Military Assistance

US and Australian defense interests are strongly linked through the ANZUS mutual security treaty. We have already offered evidence that the United States has no more reliable ally than Australia. Congress recognized the closeness of the Australian-American relationship by granting Australia the same favored treatment afforded our NATO Allies when it amended the Arms Export Control Act (PL 97–133) in 1982.

Naturally then, the United States should include Australia in plans for defense of the Indian Ocean (especially the eastern approaches). We should offer appropriate levels of military assistance to ensure that Australia becomes a capable partner in carrying out these plans. The United States has already adopted a liberal technology sharing policy with Australia.[28] And within the limits of its resources, Australia has modernized its forces considerably.[29] Recent purchases include 4 FFG frigates, 75 F/A–18 fighters and 10 P–3C LRMP aircraft. If we desire or expect the Australians to perform missions in the Indian Ocean such as SLOC protection and sea control, then we must consider assisting them to ensure a meaningful defense capability in the region. Nothing would contribute more to that goal than to help Australia obtain a proper aircraft carrier.

Australia's effort to replace HMAS *Melbourne* has been extensively reported.[30] The consensus from the outset has been that airpower is critical to a nation's defense; and to a maritime nation such as Australia, the case for airpower over the surrounding seas was overwhelming. Australia originally favored a carrier because of the unique advantages of its operational versatility, defendability, and mobility, and the political flexibility inherent in naval forces.[31]

Britain's experience in the Falkland Islands War reinforced the Fraser government's resolve to acquire a carrier. But it also forced Britain to withdraw the offer to sell HMS *Invincible*, Australia's best hope for obtaining a carrier at an affordable cost. Australia was weighing other carrier procurement options, which were gravitating toward some sort of vertical/short takeoff and landing (V/STOL) aircraft carrier, either used or new. But where *Invincible* at $478 million was palatable, a new US-designed LPH-class light carrier was hard to justify; and it invited a reopening of the whole question of need.[32]

The United States has a stake in the carrier decision. In an era when the United States cannot meet its peacetime carrier commitments except through contrivances such as FLEXOPS, we need to encourage our allies to augment our carrier forces where possible. In support of Australia's search for a light carrier, the United States has proposed four designs, ranging in cost from $1.4 billion to $2.2 billion (1982 US dollars). Each design would be capable of operating V/STOL aircraft; the most costly design also would be able to operate F/A–18 (fighter-attack), E–2C (early warning), and SH–60 (antisubmarine warfare, or ASW) aircraft.[33] However, when (and indeed if, given the ALP's rejection of the idea) Australia decides to purchase a carrier, it will probably choose lower cost rather than greater capability. This will be true as long as the current domestic economic and political climate exists.

To assist Australia in providing a common defense in the Indian Ocean, the United States should offer to transfer or favorably lease to the RAN an *Essex*-class carrier presently in the US reserve fleet. In 1981, the US Navy estimated it would take 34 months and $503 million (excluding an air wing) to return the USS *Oriskany* to service.[34] Of the $503 million, $170 million was to make the ship seaworthy and $333 million was for modernization.[35] Subsequent studies indicated that the USS *Bon Homme Richard* was in better material condition and, thus, a better candidate for refurbishment; but costs were not estimated.[36] When the two nuclear aircraft carriers were approved in the FY83 budget, the US Navy dropped the idea of bringing an *Essex*-class ship out of mothballs. These ships are under no claim now save a wartime contingency role, which seems implausible in light of the 34 months required to make them ready for service.

Irrespective of Australia's decision, the idea of helping Australia acquire an *Essex*-class carrier as the centerpiece of its fleet is certainly favorable from a US perspective for several reasons.

A carrier oriented fleet would be a great asset in performing the roles and missions expected of Australia in wartime. While a V/STOL-capable design would suffice, a conventional carrier unquestionably provides the best mix of power projection, self-protection (early warning and ASW), and survivability. Some observers point to the success of the British Sea Harrier V/STOL aircraft in the Falklands War as evidence that V/STOL carriers and aircraft are adequate for projecting power at sea. However, the British fleet suffered heavily because it never gained air superiority. The Sea Harriers handled themselves well in one-on-one engagements. But the V/STOL carrier task force could not prevent Argentine aircraft from penetrating British defenses and releasing their ordnance against the Royal Navy's ships. Thus, a conventional carrier in its fleet is the best way for Australia to put fighting power to sea.

Given the formidable presence of an Australian carrier in the Indian Ocean, the United States could lower its commitment there. Perhaps the RAN could periodically relieve one of the US CVBGs. The capability of Australian naval assets to supplant those of the United States would be especially beneficial when a crisis elsewhere in the world required redirection of US resources.

In addition, the US Navy is phasing out surplus A-4 and A-7 aircraft from its inventory. The availability of these aircraft would let Australia provide an air wing for a conventional carrier relatively quickly and economically.

Finally, and not to be overlooked, assisting an old and trusted ally in this way would create lasting good will and friendship. Transferring a carrier would be especially salutary if timed to coincide with the Australian Commonwealth Centennial in 1988.

The idea of transferring an *Essex*-class carrier is not without its drawbacks. Cost is the obvious problem. Also, Australia anticipated replacing HMAS *Melbourne* with a ship requiring about the same manpower (1200 men) [37] while an *Essex*-class ship requires up to 2090 men, or 3200 men including the air wing.[38] On the other hand, Australia would have 3 years to build up the additional manpower if needed. Also, as happened when the USS *New Jersey* was returned to service, reductions in command and control and ship defenses could significantly reduce the designed manning requirements.

Technical Transfer and Cooperation

The limited resources that the United States and Australia can devote to defense of the Indian Ocean restrict the two countries' ability to cooperate in the task. A limited population and a modest economic base constrain Australia's total defense budget, while US efforts in the region must contend with the realities of worldwide commitments.

One way to increase the Australian-American capability in the Indian Ocean would be for Australia to provide more resources, both for its own defense and for support of joint objectives. But Australian defense spending is rigidly defined by domestic political considerations and GDP. As an alternative, Australia could increase the capability of its armed forces by procuring and supporting weapons more efficiently. Australia's efforts since World War II toward greater self-sufficiency in defense equipment may be too expensive to continue.

As a principal supplier of Australian weapons, the United States works very closely with Australia to assure equity in all arms contracts and to guarantee a source of spare parts and technical support. The two nations signed a Memorandum of Understanding (MOU) on logistics support in March 1980. In it, the United States pledged to "make its best endeavours [sic] to provide assistance sought by Australia" in meeting the latter country's logistics needs in peace and war.[39] These words have not totally reassured the Australians, who have continued their efforts to be as self-sufficient as possible in defense material. But the Canberra government is realistic enough to recognize the limits of Australian defense industrial capability; rather than attempt to provide all material needs of the armed services from domestic sources, it has aimed for a reasonable level of local support for major weapon systems as well as on-shore manufacture of all high-usage munitions.[40]

Where oversea purchase of a weapon is deemed advisable, the government of Australia insists that an Australian Industrial Participation (AIP) plan be part of any competing proposal. This is an effort to keep the domestic industrial base active and current. Under guidance established by the Australians in 1970, 30 percent of the price of any major acquisition must be included as AIP offsets; offsets can take the form of designated (directly related to the weapon being purchased) or nondesignated (not project related but at a comparable level of technology) work.[41] The Australian government subsidizes the added cost associated with establishing the offset. In many cases, the contract is executed only with the contractor's promise to do everything possible to secure the desired level of AIP. History shows that the actual offsets often have not met the 30 percent goal.[42]

The effort to provide a high level of industrial self-reliance and the relatively low level of offsets gained with foreign weapon purchases are placing a heavy burden on Australian defense budgets. Australia must pay a penalty to maintain a relatively small force and to establish offset production capability. And because desired offset levels are not met, the industry does not gain the additional economic activity that would have been generated. As the largest weapon supplier to Australia, the United States needs to take the lead in remedying this situation and allowing the Australian government to provide more defense capability from its limited budget.

Both sides of the Pacific can help improve the efficiency of Australian logistics. The Australians can drive a harder bargain in establishing guaranteed offsets as a part of major weapon contracts. Promises of future offset work are not enough; the contractor must provide actual offset work or agree to pay monetary concessions if such offsets are not forthcoming before delivery of the weapons. Also, Australia needs to identify its weapon requirements earlier. Then its industry can qualify as a supplier of components for an entire production run rather than for just those units going to Australia. This would sustain the level of work and would reduce costs through efficiency and the spreading of sunk costs over a larger base. Here the United States can help by coordinating with Australia on coming weapon development programs more closely than the 1980 logistics MOU calls for.

The US Department of Defense can also take the lead in promoting regional cooperation for production and support of weapon systems. The scope of this essay does not permit detailed discussion of this point, but we can provide a basic outline. The United States should invite friendly industrialized nations in the Pacific region (Japan, Korea, Australia, New Zealand, and perhaps Malaysia and Singapore) to join a Pacific Armaments Coordination Council (PACC). The council would help provide mutual cooperation in the production and support of common weapons from the earliest possible moment. Where common requirements exist, the interested countries can form a consortium for development, production, and support, as our NATO Allies did for the F–16.

For example, Korea, Japan, and Australia are all purchasing modern fighter aircraft (F–16, F–15, and F/A–18, respectively); the last two countries will assemble their aircraft domestically. Had these three nations selected a common design, they might have been able to negotiate higher percentages of offset production, secure a greater regional support capability, and still assemble their own aircraft. Similarly, New Zealand, Australia, and Japan all purchased or are purchasing P–3 Orion LRMP aircraft, with Japan undertaking coproduction. Here again, regional cooperation would have been economically beneficial to all concerned.

The list of weapons and country combinations is limitless, but a mechanism for discussion at an early stage—the PACC—is essential. Since the United States sells weapons to all these countries, it would be a logical leader in such an effort. Obviously, considerations of US security and domestic employment would limit this scheme somewhat. But even partial implementation can do much to foster allied interoperability and improved military capability at minimum cost.[43]

US Land-Based Air Presence

The Australian government has granted the United States permission to operate B-52 bombers over training routes in northern and western Australia. It also has granted use of Darwin as a staging base for these training flights and for surveillance flights over the Indian Ocean. Beginning in 1981, the surveillance missions have provided an important new US capability in the region. In addition to furnishing information on the movement of Soviet and other forces in the Indian Ocean, the flights give aircrews experience that will be invaluable in time of crisis or conflict. These periodic B-52 flights also graphically demonstrate Western presence and resolve in the region.

The Australian press has reported that Australia has authorized up to 16 of these surveillance or training missions every month. But Major General Ruben Autry, USAF, commander of the SAC 3rd Air Division on Guam, has stated publicly that an average of only one surveillance mission per quarter is actually flown.[44] The United States should take greater advantage of the opportunity to operate B-52 LRMP missions and their supporting tanker aircraft missions from Darwin or other Australian bases. Such missions would give more US aircrews experience in the region, and a higher sustained tempo of operations would promote greater acceptance of such activity during a crisis or time of rising tension. Australian citizens are sensitive to the US presence on their soil. To assure needed freedom of action in all situations, our government needs to do everything possible to promote a business-as-usual appearance to our operations.

The staging of US Navy P-3 Orions at airfields in western or northern Australia could produce the same benefits as operating B-52 LRMP missions from Australian bases. The P-3 is already in service with the RAAF. It is well suited to its LRMP and ASW roles over the Indonesian archipelago and straits and the sea approaches to Australia. In the event of a crisis in the Indian Ocean, the US Navy would also require unimpeded access to these waters. That access may demand more resources than are available in the small force of Australian LRMP aircraft. The US

Navy may have to operate its own P–3 aircraft in some strength in the region, and Australian bases would prove invaluable.

The US government should work closely with the Australian government to agree on regular deployments of US Navy P–3 detachments (approximately three aircraft and four crews) to bases in northern or western Australia (Darwin and Learmouth being the most favorable choices). Such operations could use the same *modus operandi* as the B–52 surveillance flights—the aircraft deploying to a base, conducting operations for a period of time, then returning to their home base.

A permanent operating location to support detachments on deployment from their home base would be more valuable to joint Australian-American defense cooperation. The operation would involve a permanent cadre of perhaps a few dozen maintenance and administrative personnel to support the deployed aircraft and crews. The location should have a stock of high-use spare parts to permit a limited maintenance capability. The operating location could be an all-US Navy operation with the capability of supporting RAAF Orions as needed; or it could be a jointly manned and funded facility with a more formally scheduled mix of RAAF and US Navy deployments. The P–3C aircraft common to the two services would facilitate such joint operations and support.

US Navy participation in a project of this nature would, like the B–52 deployments, provide valuable aircrew experience while creating a visible and credible presence in the region. The establishment of a joint use LRMP base in northern or western Australia would enhance RAAF maritime capability in the Indian Ocean and the Indonesian archipelago. Thus, it would help our ally realize a long-stated defense objective. The increase in personnel and flight activity to support such an operation would have positive economic impact on the area of the base. This would be in keeping with the desires of the Australian government to encourage development in northern and western Australia. The relatively small number of permanently assigned US personnel involved with such an operating location would not politically offend the Australians. No military aircraft would be permanently based in Australia, and the aircraft participating in such deployments would be visibly similar to Australian aircraft operating from the same base. These facts further promote the acceptability of such an arrangement.

We see no overriding need to permanently base US air assets in Australia. While the movement of large numbers of people and resources into an underdeveloped area would have a positive economic impact, such a move would make Australian-American defense cooperation a political issue; and the ALP has already taken a clear public stand against American bases in their country. Also, the United States would be hard-pressed to find funds for developing a major base in an already over-extended defense budget.

The present arrangements for operating US aircraft through Australian bases appear to be working quite well. So long as Australia permits us to continue this practice, US forces can remain deployed as they are and still retain the option of operating from Australian bases as the need arises. The United States should take every opportunity to use Australian bases, particularly with LRMP and tanker assets, and to exercise regularly in close cooperation with Australian forces to enhance mutual capabilities in the region.

Regional Diplomacy and Military Cooperation

Australia has played an impressive diplomatic role in the Indian Ocean region in recent years, and the United States should encourage continued activity. Perhaps most important, Australia injects a Western perspective into regional affairs. The Australians have worked particularly well with Indonesia, Malaysia, and Singapore, all of which can play important roles in any Indian Ocean drama. The newly elected ALP government may somewhat change Australia's policy on the Indian Ocean Zone of Peace. We should try to foster an Australian viewpoint compatible with our own. However, even if an unfavorable change on the Zone of Peace should occur, we should not lose sight of Australia's overall diplomatic worth to us.

Australian participation in the Five Power Defense Arrangement and the cooperation it provides for Singapore and Malaysia has great value.[45] We should quietly encourage its continuation. The Australian P-3 detachment at Butterworth Air Station merits special mention for its surveillance and ASW capability. The Australian government is withdrawing its Mirage fighter units from Butterworth for refitting with F/A-18s.[46] No decision has been made to return F/A-18 units to Malaysia; but such a deployment would be desirable, both in terms of force projection and as a sign of Western interest. The United States should encourage it. Australian participation in the Sinai Multinational Force has also been most valuable. We should strive to convince the Hawke government to maintain it.

Australian military assistance in the region is limited but meaningful, both in practical and symbolic terms. Australian military assistance totaled $A35 million in 1982, the largest recipients being Papua New Guinea, Indonesia, and Malaysia.[47] The United States exchanges assistance information with Australia, but the two countries do not coordinate their military assistance programs in advance. To do so would be useful and cost-effective, especially with respect to countries of special importance to Australia. This is yet another domain in which joint planning would make sense and in which a stronger ANZUS structure might play a role.

Australia has managed well the question of the future status of the Cocos Islands, thereby defusing a potential uproar in the United Nations. Having bought out the interests of the British owner, Canberra is permitting the small, largely ethnic Malay local community to freely decide its own future. The Australians have, however, made it clear to the inhabitants that their best economic option is integration with Australia.[48] The islands have strategic value in support of allied Indian Ocean ASW operations; one hopes they will still be available for that role after the self-determination process. Perhaps the most important element of all is to prevent Soviet presence or influence.

Encouraging a Stronger Australian Defense Budget

In 1982 the Australian defense budget totaled $A4.1 billion, about 2.7 percent of GDP.[49] Prime Minister Fraser's program to increase defense spending in real terms by 7 percent a year for 5 years starting in 1979 reflected his own view that the commitment to defense was inadequate. The percentage of Australian GDP dedicated to security has increased slightly but is still less than half the comparable US figure.

Australians, like many other allies, are reluctant to increase defense spending; their economy is in difficulty, the threat seems remote, and any additional contribution they can make seems negligible when compared to US or Soviet military might. They, like many of our allies, sometimes fail to appreciate that the combined effort adds substantially to allied flexibility and capability; and perhaps even more important, combined effort signals resolve to the Soviet Union and its surrogates. In the case of Australia, increased expenditures could address countless gaps. These gaps include force structure, major acquisitions (including an aircraft carrier), logistic support, and secure communications equipment compatible with ours.

Obviously, the Australian government must decide how it will shape and equip its armed forces. We should not, however, shrink from reminding the Australians (and our other allies) that they, too, must carry a fair share of the mutual defense burden. We should not downplay what Australia is doing already in terms of providing facilities and attempting to modernize. But we should encourage further progress.

CONCLUSIONS

Australians and Americans have a unique relationship. This is due to shared political, social, and economic aspirations as well as a frontier experience that has profoundly affected national development and outlook. The two countries have worked closely to strengthen the free world and have fought to defend common security interests. The United States accepts the global responsibilities inherent in the leadership of the free world. And realizing its own limitations, the United States looks to allies such as Australia to play an increased role in regional affairs.

The Indian Ocean is, in fact, a perfect example of an area where available US forces are stretched beyond acceptable limits. Australian-American cooperation is already at a high level, but much more can be done. A stronger, more vigilant Australia is in the interest of Australia, America, and the entire free world. It is not only a question of encouraging Australia to devote more of its resources to security requirements, although that is part of the answer. We also must plan and work together more closely to ensure a cost-effective deterrent to aggression.

Basic Australian-American interests are so similar that partisan politics should not affect them. Strategies to achieve fundamental objectives will vary, however, depending on political developments in Canberra and Washington. The results of the 5 March 1983 Australian election will, therefore, influence the way the US government implements any part of the program suggested by this essay.

The United States should not seek any significant changes in the form or substance of the current relationship for several months. Prime Minister Hawke will need time to consolidate his position and will give priority to domestic issues. ALP rhetoric has called for review of various aspects of our defense arrangements, and Hawke must take this into account. But such a review seems unlikely to cause any essential change in the substance of our bilateral relationship or in the current level of cooperation. During the new government's initial phase, Washington should expect minor adjustments in Australian foreign or defense policy. These will be intended to satisfy certain elements in the party and underscore the change in government.

A good starting point on the path to greater cooperation would be to improve consultations. We might carefully take an initiative in this area during the early days of the new government. The ALP leadership may well appreciate an invitation of this type for domestic political reasons. Likewise, they may appreciate the opportunity to place Australian representatives at CENTCOM and PACOM to improve military liaison. We should take advantage of contacts with senior officials in the new government to encourage them to look beyond a "fortress Australia" approach to security matters.

After sufficient time, other initiatives that clearly promise a net gain to Australia might be appropriate. Greater use of HMAS Stirling by US Navy vessels and an arrangement for larger naval fueling facilities in the Perth area would help build up valuable Australian-owned and -controlled security infrastructure at reduced cost to Australia. Development of regional coproduction of defense items is a more complex and long term issue; but coproduction would certainly benefit Australia by reducing unit costs, creating jobs, and enhancing prestige in the region.

Reasonably early, we should also encourage Australia to continue an active defense role vis-a-vis important neighbors, and we should offer to coordinate more closely on military assistance to those nations. Continued Five Power participation is especially important. The replacement of Mirage fighters with F/A–18s at Butterworth appears less likely under Hawke than under Fraser; but we should do what we can to convince the new government of the value of such a deployment.

On other, more controversial initiatives, we must take a wait-and-see attitude. For example, the timing of a strong pitch for increasing the share of Australian GDP devoted to defense expenditures will depend on many factors—but it should be made, and relatively soon. The recent indications that Hawke will bolster the defense budget may make this less controversial than might have been anticipated before the election.

Some ALP members, because they advocate a more independent defense posture, might see joint planning as politically controversial. Nonetheless, the new government may be able to put rhetoric aside and accept as logical and beneficial our proposal, presented as we described earlier, for limited joint planning in the eastern Indian Ocean. We will have to play a passive role for the present on any change in the number or form of joint exercises, ship visits, and P–3 or B–52 missions. We hope that the Hawke government will pose no obstacle to continuing or eventually increasing such activities. We should defer any suggestions to add to current agreements (for example, by increasing P–3 or B–52 missions or by organizing an ANZUS secretariat) until the new government has settled into office.

The proposal to assist Australia in obtaining an aircraft carrier is the most doubtful of all. Hawke has confirmed earlier ALP statements opposing the acquisition of a carrier. Short of a dramatic change in the security situation, he is unlikely to entertain the idea of investing any Australian funds in such a venture. The United States should not push hard on this issue. On the other hand, an Australian fleet with a carrier at its heart would significantly benefit all involved. It is worth proposing at the right moment.

This essay has outlined modest but concrete ways to improve allied capabilities, infrastructure, and cooperation in the Indian Ocean to meet US goals in the region. These suggestions take into account fiscal realities of both the United States and Australia and possible public relations problems. Most of the proposals are noncontroversial. The authors believe the two governments can obtain public approval for all these measures without great difficulty if the will to do so exists. We see no serious international opposition to a strengthening of an already existing alliance.

On a global basis, the time has come to reexamine the importance of continued survival of the free world and the contribution each of its members must make to ensure that survival. In many ways, our relationship with Australia is less in need of improvement than our relationship with other friends. So perhaps Australia is a good starting place for a broad revitalization of free world vigilance.

ENDNOTES

Operation Barbarossa

1. Winston S. Churchill, *Their Finest Hour* (Boston: Houghton Mifflin Co., 1949), p. 115.

2. Lynn Montross, *War Through the Ages,* 3d ed. (New York: Harper & Brothers Publishers, 1960), p. 842.

3. H.R. Trevor-Roper, *Blitzkrieg to Defeat* (New York: Holt, Rinehart and Winston, 1964), p. 212.

4. Ibid., p. 49.

5. Lucien Zacharoff, *We Made A Mistake—Hitler* (New York: D. Appleton-Century Co., 1941), p. 86.

6. Ibid., p. 83.

7. Carl von Clausewitz, *On War,* translated and edited by Michael Howard and Peter Paret (Princeton, New Jersey: Princeton University Press, 1976), p. 85.

8. Montross, *War Through the Ages,* p. 849.

9. Earl F. Ziemke, *Stalingrad to Berlin: The German Defeat in the East,* Army Historical Series (Washington, DC: Office of the Chief of Military History, US Army, 1968), p. 1.

10. Trevor-Roper, *Blitzkrieg to Defeat,* p. 49.

11. Clausewitz, *On War,* p. 194.

12. Alan Clark, *Barbarossa: The Russian-German Conflict, 1941–45* (New York: William Morrow and Company, 1965), p. 46.

13. Ziemke, *Stalingrad to Berlin: The German Defeat in the East,* p. 203.

14. James L. Stokesbury, *A Short History of World War II* (New York: William Morrow and Co. Inc., 1980), p. 314; and Montross, *War Through the Ages,* p. 530.

Endnotes

15. Clark, *Barbarossa: The Russian-German Conflict, 1941–45*, p. 44.

16. William L. Shirer, *The Rise and Fall of the Third Reich* (New York: Fawcett World Library, 1962), p. 1078.

17. Montross, *War Through the Ages*, p. 844.

18. Clausewitz, *On War*, p. 358.

19. Ibid.

20. Ibid., p. 628.

21. Ibid., p. 268.

22. Clark, *Barbarossa: The Russian-German Conflict, 1941–45*, p. 138.

23. Ibid., p. 42.

24. Clausewitz, *On War*, p. 628.

Tantalus Revisited

1. Remarks of George Bush, Vice President of the United States of America, at the United Nations Committee on Disarmament, Palais des Nations, Geneva, Switzerland, 4 February 1983.

2. Robert Mikulak, "The Rocky Road to a Ban on Chemical and Biological Warfare." Review of "A Higher Form of Killing: The Secret Story of Chemical and Biological Warfare," by Robert Harris and Jeremy Paxman, *Chemical and Engineering News*, 22 November 1982, p. 34.

3. US Congress, Joint Committee, *Fiscal Year 1983 Arms Control Impact Statements*, pp. 277–278.

4. General Bernard Rogers, *Statement of SACEUR before the Senate Armed Services Committee*, 1 March 1982.

5. Department of State Bulletin, Military Affairs, *US Program to Deter Chemical Warfare*, Fact Sheet, 8 February 1982, p. 58.

6. J.P. Perry Robinson, "Chemical Warfare Capabilities of the Warsaw and North Atlantic Treaty Organizations: an Overview from Open Sources," *Chemical Weapons: Destruction and Conversion*, Stockholm International Peace Research Institute, p. 39.

7. US Congress, Joint Committee, *Fiscal Year 1982 Arms Control Impact Statements*, p. XIII.

8. Quoted in Ann Van Wynen Thomas and A.J. Thomas, Jr., *Legal Limits on the Use of Chemical and Biological Weapons*, p. 44.

9. Ibid.

10. Ibid., p. 46.

11. Ibid., p. 49.

12. Ibid., p. 47.

13. Ibid., p. 65.

14. Gwendolyn M. Bedford, *The Geneva Protocol of 1925: A Case Study in the Dynamics of Political Decision and Public Opinion in Biological and Chemical Warfare*, p. 51.

15. Sterling Seagrave, *Yellow Rain*, p. 77.

16. Stockholm International Peace Research Institute, "CB Disarmament Negotiations, 1920–1970," *The Problem of Chemical and Biological Warfare*, 4:105. (Hereafter cited as SIPRI, *Problem of CBW*.)

17. Ibid., p. 145.

18. US Congress, Joint Committee, *US Arms Control and Disarmament Agency 1981 Annual Report*, p. 18.

19. United Nations, General Assembly, *Report of the Committee on Disarmament*, 1982, p. 40.

20. Ibid., p. 3.

21. US Congress, Joint Committee, *US Arms Control and Disarmament Agency 1981 Annual Report*, p. 19.

22. United Nations, General Assembly, *Report of the Committee on Disarmament*, 1982, p. 72.

23. Stockholm International Peace Research Institute, *Strategic Disarmament Verification and National Security*, p. 13.

24. Ibid., p. 33.

25. Ibid., p. 34.

26. Department of State, *Chemical Warfare in Southeast Asia and Afghanistan*, Special Report No. 98, 22 March 1982.

27. Ambassador Lawrence S. Eagleburger, *Statement of the Undersecretary of State for Political Affairs before the Arms Control, Oceans, International Operations and Environment Subcommittee of the Senate Foreign Relations Committee*, 24 February 1983.

28. USSR, *Basic Provisions of a Convention on the Prohibition of the Development, Production and Stockpiling of Chemical Weapons and on Their Destruction*, CD/294, 21 July 1982, p. 6.

29. Ibid., p. 7.

30. Ibid., p. 8.

31. Ibid.

32. United States, *US Detailed Views on the Contents of a Chemical Weapons Ban*, 10 February 1983, p. 13.

33. Ibid., p. 16.

34. Mikulak, p. 35.

35. Remarks by Ambassador Louis G. Fields, Jr., before the Committee on Disarmament, Geneva, Switzerland, 10 February 1983.

36. SIPRI, "Technical Aspects of Early Warning and Verification," *Problem of CBW*, 6:254.

37. Midwest Research Institute, *Studies on the Technical Arms Control Aspects of Chemical and Biological Warfare*, 1:12.

38. John Lundin, *Considerations on a Chemical Arms Control Treaty and the Concept of Amplified Verification*, p. 2. See also SIPRI, *Problem of CBW*, 5:189.

39. Ibid.

40. Matthew Meselson and Julian Perry Robinson, "Chemical Warfare and Chemical Disarmament," *Scientific American*, April 1980, p. 47.

41. SIPRI, "The Prevention of CBW," *Problem of CBW*, 5:115.

42. Nickolas A. Sims, "Britain, Chemical Weapons and Disarmament," *ADIU Report*, Vol. 2, No. 3 (July/August 1980), p. 1–F.

43. S.J. Lundin, "Confidence-Building Measures and a Chemical Weapons Convention," *Chemical Weapons: Destruction and Conversion*, Stockholm International Peace Research Institute, p. 139.

Deep Attack in Defense of Central Europe

1. Phillip A. Karber, "To Lose an Arms Race: The Competition in Conventional Forces Deployed in Central Europe, 1965–1980," unpublished research paper (Washington, DC: October 1981), pp. 64–67. C.N. Donnelly, "Tactical Problems Facing the Soviet Army: Recent Debates in the Soviet Military Press," *International Defense Review*, September 1976, pp. 1405–1412.

2. Robert S. Cooper, "The Coming Revolution in Conventional Weapons," *Astronautics and Aeronautics*, October 1982, pp. 74–75; Benjamin F. Schemmer, "NATO's New Strategy: Defend Forward, But Strike Deep," *Armed Forces Journal International*, November 1982, p. 59.

3. Headquarters, Dept. of the Army, *Operations*, Field Manual 100–5 (Washington, DC: 1982), p. 1–1.

4. Ibid., pp. 7–1 through 7–17.

5. Ibid., p. 7–15.

6. Ibid., p. 7–11.

7. Interview with Col. Kenneth Keller, Special Assistant to the Chief of Staff, Supreme Headquarters, Allied Powers Europe (SHAPE), Belgium, 9 February 1983.

8. *The Daily Telegraph*, 1 November 1982, p. 18. Quoted in *Foreign Broadcast Information Service (FBIS)*, 12 November 1982.

9. Benjamin F. Schemmer, "NATO's New Strategy: Defend Forward, But Strike Deep," *Armed Forces Journal International*, November 1982, p. 51.

10. General Meinhard Glanz, interview in *Stern*, 11 November 1982, pp. 294–307. Quoted in *FBIS*, 15 November 1982.

11. Speech by General Bernard W. Rogers, Supreme Commander, Allied Powers Europe, Brussels, September 1982.

12. *Le Monde*, "A New Atlantic Strategy," 5 October 1982. Quoted in *FBIS*, 7 October 1982, p. 1.

13. McGeorge Bundy, et al, "Nuclear Weapons and the Atlantic Alliance, *Foreign Affairs*, Spring 1982.

14. Robert S. Cooper, "The Coming Revolution in Conventional Weapons," *Astronautics and Aeronautics*, October 1982, p. 74.

15. David S. Yost and Thomas C. Glad, "West German Party Politics and Theater Nuclear Modernization Since 1977," *Armed Forces and Society*, Summer 1982, p. 328.

16. Walter Pincus, "Army Would Like Advance Authority to Use A–Weapons," *Washington Post*, July 21, 1982; also, "US Military Wants Decisions on Nuclear Weapons," *Sueddeutsche Zeitung*, 22 July 1982.

17. Glanz, op. cit.

18. Headquarters, Dept. of the Army, *Operations*, Field Manual 100–5 (Washington, DC: 1982).

19. Col. Bud Adair, US Army, "Airland Battle Briefing," Fort Monroe, Va., US Army Training and Doctrine Command, November 1982.

20. Information about the organization and deployment of WTO forces used here represents a synthesis from several sources listed in the bibliography, most notably Cordier, Dupuy, Isby, Menaul, Weiner, and the IISS annual balance studies.

21. US Dept. of Defense, *Soviet Military Power: 1983* (Washington: 1983).

22. US Dept. of Defense, Defense Intelligence Agency, *Soviet Divisional Organizational Guide*, July 1982 (DDB-1100-333-82).

23. C.N. Donnelly, "The Soviet Operational Manoeuvre Group: A New Challenge for NATO," *International Defense Review*, September 1982, pp. 1177-1186. Aleksander Musial (Colonel, Polish Air Force), "Air Force Combat Operations on Behalf of Operational Maneuver Groups," Defense Intelligence Agency Translation LN-595-82, from *Przeglad Wojsk Lotniczych I Wojsk Obrony Powietrznej Kraju*, 1982.

24. US Dept. of Defense, *The FY 1984 Department of Defense Program for Research, Development, and Acquisition* (Washington: 1983), p. II-19.

25. Ibid., p. I-10.

26. *Aviation Week & Space Technology*, 1 November 1982, p. 77.

27. *Aviation Week & Space Technology*, 19 July 1982, pp. 141-143.

28. Ibid.

29. *Aviation Week & Space Technology*, 1 November 1982, p. 77.

30. Ibid.

31. Ibid.

32. Ibid., p. 78.

33. US Dept. of Defense, *FY 1984 Report of Secretary of Defense Caspar W. Weinberger to the Congress*, 1 February 1983, p. 251.

34. *Defense Electronics*, January 1983, pp. 74-80.

35. Op. cit., Weinberger FY 1984 Report, p. 137.

36. Ibid., p. 251.

37. Ibid., p. 250.

38. *Aviation Week & Space Technology*, 7 June 1982, pp. 64-67.

39. Ibid.

40. Ibid.

41. *Aviation Week & Space Technology*, 20 September 1982, pp. 117-125.

42. *Aviation Week & Space Technology*, 22 March 1982, pp. 66-69.

43. US Dept. of Defense, Defense Intelligence Agency, *Handbook of Economic Statistics* (Washington: 1982), p. 53.

44. Ibid., p. 65.

45. Ibid., p. 53.

46. Benjamin F. Schemmer, "NATO's New Strategy: Defend Forward, But Strike Deep," *Armed Forces Journal*, October 1982, p. 63.

47. Ibid., p. 65.

48. William Drozdiak, "Europe Fears Prolonged Period of Stagnation," *Washington Post*, 9 January 1983, p. H1:6.

49. Ibid.

50. US Dept. of Defense, *Report on Allied Contributions to the Common Defense*, March 1982.

Atlantic Cooperation for Persian Gulf Security

1. Hans-Dietrich Genscher, "Toward an Overall Western Strategy," *Foreign Affairs*, Fall 1982, Vol. 61, No. 1, pp. 42–66.

2. James H. Noyes, *The Clouded Lens: Persian Gulf Security and U.S. Policy* (Stanford: Hoover Institute, 1982), p. 128.

3. Lawrence Freedman, "The Atlantic Crisis," *International Affairs*, Summer 1982, pp. 406–11.

4. Stephen Aitner, "The Middle East: A Chance for Europe," *International Affairs*, Summer 1980, 56:420–42.

5. US Congress, Senate, Committee on Foreign Relations, *NATO Today: The Alliance in Evolution*, Report (Washington: US Government Printing Office, 1982), p. 37.

6. The Atlantic Council's Working Group on Security Affairs, *After Afghanistan—The Long Haul: Safeguarding Security and Independence in the Third World* (Boulder: Westview, 1980), p. 55.

7. Shahram Chubin, "U.S. Security Interests in the Persian Gulf in the 1980's, *Daedalus*, Fall 1980, pp. 40–41.

8. Shahram Chubin, *Security in the Persian Gulf 4: The Role of Outside Powers* (Totowa, New Jersey: Allenheld, Osmun, 1982), p. 113.

9. Valerie Yorke, "The Gulf in the 1980's," *Chatham House Papers*, No. 6 (London: Royal Institute of International Affairs, 1980), p. VII.

10. Melvin Conant, *The Oil Factor in U.S. Policy, 1980–1990*, Council on Foreign Relations, 1982, D.C. Heath and Co., p. 29.

11. James H. Noyes, *The Clouded Lens: Persian Gulf Security and U.S. Policy* (Stanford: Hoover Institute, 1982), p. 128.

12. The Atlantic Council's Working Group on Security Affairs, *After Afghanistan*, pp. 62–63.

13. Johnson and Pacband, eds., *The Common Security Interests of Japan, The United States and NATO* (Cambridge: Ballinger, 1981), p. 35.

14. Karl Kaiser, et al., *Western Security: What Has Changed? What Should be Done?* (New York: Council on Foreign Relations, 1981), p. 33.

15. US Congress, House, Committee on Appropriations, *Southwest Asia Military Construction*, Hearings (Washington: US Government Printing Office, 8 March 1983).

16. US Congress, House, Committee on Foreign Affairs, *Soviet Policy and United States Response in The Third World*, Report by the Congressional Research Service (Washington: US Government Printing Office, 1981), pp. 241–42.

Australia, America, and Indian Ocean Security

1. The Library of Congress, Congressional Research Service, *Rapid Deployment Joint Task Force Recast As Unified Command* (Washington: US Government Printing Office, 10 December 1982).

2. Henry S. Albinski, *The Australian-American Security Relationship: A Regional and International Perspective* (St. Lucia, Queensland, Australia: University of Queensland Press, 1982), p. 116.

3. *Overseas Trade of Australia: Comparative and Summary Tables II* (Canberra: Australian Bureau of Statistics, 1982).

4. See Desmond Ball, *A Suitable Piece of Real Estate* (Sydney: Hale and Iremonger, 1980).

5. Parliament of the Commonwealth of Australia, Joint Committee on Foreign Affairs and Defense, *Threats to Australia's Security: Their Nature and Probability* (Canberra: Australian Government Publishing Service, 1981), pp. 40–42.

6. John McCarthy, "Problems in Australian Foreign Policy," *The Australian Journal of Politics and History*, December 1977, p. 337.

7. The CY 1982 inflation rate was 11 percent and GDP dropped 2 percent. Prospects for a rapid turnaround remain dim. Sources: Australian Bureau of Statistics; *The Mid-December Treasurer's Report, 1982*; and *The Melbourne University Economic Forecast for 1983*.

8. RAN 17,626; RAAF 22,707; Army 32,850. International Institute for Strategic Studies, "The Military Balance 1982/83," *Air Force Magazine*, December 1982, p. 127.

9. Rt. Hon. Ian Sinclair, Speech to The Australian Defence Association, 19 November 1982.

10. "The Hornet Keeps Its Sting," *Pacific Defence Reporter*, November 1982, p. 59.

11. VAdm Sir James Willis, RAN, "Why We Bought *Invincible*," *Pacific Defence Reporter*, April 1982, pp. 61–62.

12. A.W. Grazebrook, "After *Invincible*—Where Next?" *Pacific Defence Reporter*, September 1982, p. 32.

13. Gary Brown and Derek Woolher, *A New Aircraft Carrier for RAN?* (Canberra: Australian National University, Strategic and Defence Center, 28 July 1982).

14. Sub. Lt. J.V.P. Goldrick, RAN, and Sub. Lt. P.D. Jones, RAN, "The Royal Australian Navy—A Progress Report," *U.S. Naval Institute Proceedings*, July 1981, p. 112.

15. A.W. Grazebrook, "Australia's Maritime Airpower: Where Next?" *Pacific Defence Reporter*, July 1982, p. 10.

16. The Parliament of the Commonwealth of Australia, *Threats to Australia's Security*, p. 94 ff.

17. For a succinct description and analysis of the ANZUS Treaty, See Thomas Durell Young, *ANZUS in the Indian Ocean: Strategic Considerations* (Geneva: Institute Universitaire des Hautes Études Internationales, 1982), pp. 48–71.

18. Information based on interviews with USN OPNAV staff (OP–60).

19. Hasjim Djalal, Chairman of the Indonesian Delegation to the Law of the Sea Conference, in an address, entitled "Economic Zones: The Concept and Its Implications," to the Pacific Symposium, National Defense University, Washington, DC, 20 January 1983.

20. Alvin J. Cottrell and Robert J. Hanks, *The Military Utility of the U.S. Facilities in the Philippines* (Washington: Georgetown University Center of Strategic and International Studies, Significant Issues Series, 1980), p. 27.

21. "Phase-Out of Bases Predicted," *Washington Times*, 7 September 1982, p. 6:1–4.

22. John Edwards in the *Bulletin*, 17 June 1980; and Denis Warner in the *Melbourne Herald*, 21 July 1980. Quoted in Henry S. Albinski, "Australia and U.S. Strategy," *Current History*, April 1982, p. 151.

23. Information based on interviews with USN OPNAV staff (OP–60).

24. Ibid.

25. Interviews with staff members of the Joint Chiefs of Staff (J–5), 17 November 1982.

26. Interview with Captain James Major, USN, CINCPAC staff, 10 February 1983.

27. Interview with Mr. Robert Brand, Deputy Assistant Secretary of State, Bureau of East Asian and Pacific Affairs, 3 December 1982.

28. Interview with USN OPNAV staff (OP–63).

29. Australia ranks second only to Saudi Arabia in active foreign military sales (FMS) transactions with the United States; ibid.

30. The two sides to this issue are best covered by Gary Brown and Derek Woolner, *A New Carrier for the Royal Australian Navy?* (Canberra: Strategic and Defense Studies Center, Australian National University, Working Paper No. 57, 28 July 1982); and by VAdm Sir James Willis, RAN, "Why We Bought *Invincible*," *Pacific Defence Reporter*, April 1982, p. 61.

31. "The Case for Sea-bourne Air Power" by "Proteus," *Pacific Defence Reporter*, October 1979, p. 8.

32. *Sydney Morning Herald*, 27 August 1982, p. 2:1–4.

33. Interview with USN OPNAV staff (OP–63).

34. Captain John E. Moore, RN, FRGS, ed., *Jane's Fighting Ships* (London: Paulton House, 1982), p. 619.

35. Ibid.

36. *Essex-Class Refurbishment*, J.J. Henry Co., Inc., Report No. 2033–00, 26 October 1981.

37. Telephone conversation with Commodore John P. Snow, RAN, Attache, Embassy of Australia, Washington, DC, 8 March 1983.

38. Moore, *Jane's Fighting Ships*, p. 619.

39. *Memorandum of Understanding on Logistic Support Between the Government of Australia and the Government of the United States of America*, 18 March 1980, p. 5.

40. D.J. Killen, "The Philosophy of Australian Defense," *Pacific Defence Reporter*, June 1981, p. 6.

41. Ian Viner, "Building Up the Defense Industries," *Pacific Defence Reporter*, September 1982, p. 12.

42. David R. Griffiths, "Australia Seeks Aerospace Self-Reliance," *Aviation Week and Space Technology*, 17 March 1980, p. 44.

43. Dr. John N. Ellison, Mobilization Concepts Development Center, National Defense University, has advanced a related idea to utilize the defense industrial capability of Australia and other Pacific basin countries to augment American industry during a defense emergency. See "Hands (Defense Industrial) Across the Pacific," *Pacific Defence Reporter*, November 1982, pp. 14, 16–17.

44. Speech to Council on Northern Australia, Port Hedland, NT, 20 October 1981.

45. The Five Powers are Australia, New Zealand, the United Kingdom, Singapore, and Malaysia. For background, see Henry S. Albinski, *The Australian-American Security Relationship*, p. 88.

46. Michael Richardson, "The RAAF's Role in South-East Asia," *Pacific Defence Reporter*," October 1982, p. 47.

47. *Australian Yearbook 1981–82* (Canberra: Australian Bureau of Statistics, 1982), pp. 63–64.

48. Frank Cranston, "Defense Interests a Major Influence," *Canberra Times*, 1 December 1982, p. 13; and M. McKinnon, "McVeigh Spells Out Cocos Islands Options," *The Australian*, 30 November 1982, p. 3.

49. *Australian Yearbook 1981–82*, p. 62.

BIBLIOGRAPHIES

Operation Barbarossa

Churchill, Winston S. *Their Finest Hour*. Boston: Houghton Mifflin Co., 1949.

Clark, Alan. *Barbarossa: The Russian-German Conflict, 1941–45*. New York: William Morrow and Company, 1965.

Clausewitz, Carl von. *On War*, translated and edited by Michael Howard and Peter Paret. Princeton, New Jersey: Princeton University Press, 1976.

Montross, Lynn. *War Through the Ages*. 3d ed. New York: Harper & Brothers Publishers, 1960.

Shirer, William L. *The Rise and Fall of the Third Reich*. New York: Fawcett World Library, 1962.

Stokesbury, James L. *A Short History of World War II*. New York: William Morrow and Co. Inc., 1980.

Turney, Alfred W. *Disaster at Moscow: Von Bock's Campaigns 1941–45*. Albuquerque, New Mexico: University of New Mexico Press, 1970.

Trevor-Roper, H.R. *Blitzkrieg to Defeat*. New York: Holt, Rinehart and Winston, 1964.

Van Creveld, Martin. "The German Attack on the USSR: The Destruction of a Legend." *European Studies Review 2* (No. I, 1972). (Printed in Great Britain.)

Zacharoff, Lucien. *We Made a Mistake—Hitler*. New York: D. Appleton-Century Co., 1941.

Ziemke, Earl F. *Stalingrad to Berlin: The German Defeat in the East*. Army Historical Series. Washington, DC: Office of the Chief of Military History, US Army, 1968.

Deep Attack in Defense of Central Europe

Adair, Col. Bud, USA, US Army Training and Doctrine Command. Interview, Ft. Monroe, Virginia, November 1982.

Aviation Week and Space Technology (22 March 1982, 7 June 1982, 19 July 1982, 20 September 1982, and 1 November 1982).

Bundy, McGeorge, et al. "Nuclear Weapons and the Atlantic Alliance." *Foreign Affairs* (Spring 1982).

Cooper, Robert S. "The Coming Revolution in Conventional Weapons." *Astronautics and Aeronautics* (October 1982).

Cordier, Sherwood S. *Calculus of Power: The Current Soviet-American Military Balance in Central Europe.* 3d ed. Washington, DC: University Press of America, 1980.

The (London) *Daily Telegraph* (1 November 1982). Quoted in *Foreign Broadcast Information Service* (hereafter, *FBIS*), 12 November 1982.

Defense Electronics (January 1983).

"Defense of Central Europe." *NATO's Fifteen Nations,* Special Issue 2 (1981).

Donnelly, C.N. "The Soviet Operational Manoeuvre Group: A New Challenge for NATO." *International Defense Review* (September 1982): 1177–1186.

Donnelly, C.N. "The Structure of the Soviet Armed Forces." *NATO's Fifteen Nations* (April-May 1980): 94–96.

Donnelly, C.N. "Tactical Problems Facing the Soviet Army: Recent Debates in the Soviet Military Press." *International Defense Review* (September 1976): 1405–1412.

Drozdiak, William. "Europe Fears Prolonged Period of Stagnation." *The Washington Post* (9 January 1983): H1:6.

Dupuy, T.N. "The New Debate: NATO's Deep Strike—Strategy for Victory or Defeat?" Unpublished article submitted to *Armed Forces Journal International,* 1982.

Dupuy, T.N. "The Soviet Second Echelon: Is This a Red Herring?" *Armed Forces Journal International* (August 1982): 60–64. Backup documentation by Col. Dupuy: "The Soviet Second Echelon: A Simulation Test," 8 pp.

Dupuy, T.N. "US Defense Budgets—The Right Priorities?" *Armed Forces Journal International* (April 1982): 91–93.

Glanz, General Meinhard. Interview in *Stern* (11 November 1982): 294–307. Quoted in *FBIS*, 15 November 1982.

Hudson Institute. *Defending NATO-Europe: Forward Defense and Nuclear*

Strategy. Report for Defense Nuclear Agency (DNA 4567F), November 1977.

International Institute for Strategic Studies. *The Military Balance, 1982–1983*. London: 1982.

Isby, David C. *Weapons and Tactics of the Soviet Army*. London: Janes, 1981.

Karber, Phillip A. "To Lose an Arms Race: The Competition in Conventional Forces Deployed in Central Europe, 1965–1980." Unpublished research paper. Washington, DC: October 1981. Interview, Washington, DC, December 1982.

Keller, Col. Kenneth, USAF, Special Assistant to the Chief of Staff, Supreme Headquarters, Allied Powers Europe (SHAPE). Interview, Belgium, 9 February 1983.

Menaul, Air Vice-Marshal Stewart. *Russian Military Power*. New York: St. Martin's Press, 1980.

Musial, Col. Aleksander. "Air Force Combat Operations on Behalf of Operational Maneuver Groups." Defense Intelligence Agency Translation LN 595–82 (from *Przeglad Wojsk Lotniczych I Wojsk Obrony Powietrznej Kraju*, no. 7–8).

"A New Atlantic Strategy." *Le Monde* (5 October 1982). Quoted in *FBIS*, 7 October 1982.

Pincus, Walter. "Army Would Like Advance Authority to Use A-Weapons." *The Washington Post* (21 July 1982). Also, "US Military Wants Decisions on Nuclear Weapons." *Sueddeutsche Zeitung* (22 July 1982).

Rogers, General Bernard W., USA, Supreme Commander, Allied Powers Europe. Speech in Brussels, Belgium, September 1982.

Schemmer, Benjamin F. "NATO's New Strategy: Defend Forward, But Strike Deep." *Armed Forces Journal International* (November 1982): 51 ff.

Schemmer, Benjamin F. "Will NATO's C³/EW/I Systems Let Its 'Strike Deep' Strategy Work?" *Armed Forces Journal International* (December 1982): 68 ff.

Schwartzman, Stewart K. *Soviet Military Strategy in Western Europe in the 1970s*. Manhattan: Kansas State University Press, 1979.

Scott, Harriet F., and William F. Scott. *The Armed Forces of the USSR*. Boulder: Westview Press, 1979.

Scott, Harriet F., and William F. Scott, eds. *The Soviet Art of War: Doctrine, Strategy, and Tactics*. Boulder: Westview Press, 1982.

Shapley, Deborah. "The Army's New Fighting Doctrine." *New York Times Magazine* (28 November 1982): 37 ff.

Siderenko, Col. A.A. *The Offensive*. Moscow: 1970. US Air Force Translation, *Soviet Military Thought* series.

US Army. *Field Manual 100-5, Operations*. Washington, DC: Headquarters, Dept. of the Army, 1983.

US Army Intelligence and Threat Analysis Center. *Soviet and United States Division Comparison Handbook*. Washington, DC: Headquarters, Dept. of the Army, 1978 (IAG-35-U-78).

US Army Intelligence and Threat Analysis Center. *Soviet Army Operations*. Washington, DC: Headquarters, Dept. of the Army, April 1978 (IAG-13-U-78).

US Army Intelligence and Threat Analysis Center. *Soviet Army Operations and Tactics*. Coordinating draft, FM 100-2-1, August 1982.

US Army War College. *Military Strategy: Theory and Application*. Carlisle Barracks: US Army War College, 1982. The following articles in this collection were of value: "Nuclear War in Suburbia: Dilemmas of Force Modernization in NATO's Center," by Gary L. Guertner; "Soviet Military Doctrine and Strategy," by (Soviet) Deputy Defense Minister S. Ivanov; and "Military Strategy," by (Soviet) Marshal N.V. Ogarkov.

US Defense Intelligence Agency. *Soviet Divisional Organizational Guide*. Washington, DC: US Department of Defense, July 1982 (DDB-1100-333-82).

US Defense Intelligence Agency. *Soviet Air Support to Ground Troops*. Washington, DC: US Department of Defense, June 1979 (DDB-1300-147-79).

US Defense Intelligence Agency. *Soviet Tactics: The Meeting Engagement*. Washington, DC: US Department of Defense, December 1976 (DDI-1100-143-76).

US Defense Intelligence Agency. *Handbook of Economic Statistics*. Washington, DC: US Department of Defense, 1982.

US Department of Defense. *The FY 1984 Department of Defense Program for Research, Development, and Acquisition*. Washington, DC: 1983.

US Department of Defense. *FY 84 Report of Secretary of Defense Caspar W. Weinberger to the Congress*. Washington, DC: 1 February 1983.

US Department of Defense. *Report on Allied Contributions to the Common Defense*. Washington, DC: March 1983.

US Department of Defense. *Soviet Military Power: 1983*. Washington, DC: 1983.

Yost, David S., and Thomas C. Glad. "West German Party Politics and Theater Nuclear Modernization Since 1977." *Armed Forces and Society* (Summer 1982): 328.

Weiner, Friedrich. *The Armies of the Warsaw Pact Nations.* Vienna: Carl Ueberreuter Publishers, 1976.

Atlantic Cooperation for Persian Gulf Security

Atlantic Council. *After Afghanistan—The Long Haul: Safeguarding Security and Independence in the Third World.* Boulder, Colorado: 1980.

Bax, Frans R. "Energy Security in the 80's." *Energy and National Security.* Washington, DC: National Defense University, 1980.

Bowie, Robert R. "The Atlantic Alliance." *Daedalus* (Winter 1981).

Bull, Hedley. "A New Course for Britain and Western Europe." *SAIS Review* (Spring 1982).

Butcher, Capt. Paul, US Navy, Director, Washington Liaison Office, Rapid Deployment Joint Task Force. Interview, 20 October 1982.

Calleo, David P. "The Atlantic Alliance: An Enduring Relationship?" *SAIS Review* (Spring 1982).

Chubin, Shahran. *Security in the Persian Gulf 4: The Role of Outside Powers.* The International Institute for Strategic Studies, 1982.

Chubin, Shahran. "Soviet Policy Towards Iran and the Gulf." *Adelphi Papers No. 157.* London: International Institute for Strategic Studies, 1980.

Cohen, Eliot A. "The Long-Term Crisis of the Alliance." *Foreign Affairs* (Winter 1982–83).

Conant, Melvin. "The Oil Factor in U.S. Foreign Policy, 1980–1990." *Council on Foreign Relations.* Lexington Books, 1982.

Cordesman, Anthony H. "Defense Burden Sharing—A Brief Scorecard on our Major Allies (And Ourselves)." *Armed Forces Journal International* (October 1982).

Cot, Jean-Pierre. "Winning East-West in North-South." *Foreign Policy* (Spring 1982).

Deese, David, and Joseph S. Nye, eds. "Energy and Security." *A Report on Harvard's Energy and Security Research Project.* Cambridge, Massachusetts: Ballinger Publishing Company, 1981.

"Defending the Gulf: A Survey." *The Economist* 279 (June 1981).

DePorte, Anton W. *Europe Between the Superpowers: The Enduring Balance.* New Haven: Yale University, 1979.

Draper, Theodore. "The Western Misalliance." *The Washington Quarterly* 4, no. 1 (Winter 1981).

Edward, Lt. Col. R.C. "The Gap in NATO Defense." Background paper for Chairman, Joint Chiefs of Staff. Washington, DC: 5 November 1980.

Freedman, Lawrence. "The Atlantic Crisis." *International Affairs* (London) 58, no. 3 (Summer 1982).

Freedman, Lawrence. "NATO Myths." *Foreign Policy* (Winter 1981/82).

Fukuyama, Francis. "New Directions for Soviet Middle East Policy in the 1980's: Implications for the Atlantic Alliance." *The Rand Paper Series*, No. P6443 (1980).

Garfinkle, Adam. "America and Europe in the Middle East." *Orbis* 25:631–48 (Fall 1981).

Gole, Henry G. *Through European Eyes: Need NATO Strategy be Changed?* Carlisle Barracks: Strategic Studies Institute, US Army War College, 1981.

Grau, Lt. Col. David, USAF, Defense Intelligence Agency, Washington, DC. Interview, 20 October 1982.

Griffith, William E. *The Superpowers and Regional Tensions: The USSR, the US and Europe.* Lexington, Maine: Lexington Books, 1981.

Grummon, Stephen R. "The Iran-Iraq War: Islam Embattled." *The Washington Papers* 92. Published with the Center for Strategic and International Studies, Georgetown University. New York: Praeger, 1982.

Haig, Alexander M., Jr. *Oil Diplomacy: The Atlantic Nations in the Oil Crisis of 1978–79.* Foreign Policy Research Institute, 1980.

Hassner, Pierre. "The Shifting Foundation." *Foreign Policy*, no. 48 (Fall 1982).

Hoffman, Stanley. "The Western Alliance: Drift or Harmony?" *International Security* (Fall 1981).

"Impact of Southwest Asia Contingencies on NATO Planning." Unpublished, 4 November 1980 (Secret).

The Impact of the Iranian Events Upon Persian Gulf and U.S. Security. American Foreign Policy Institute, 1979.

International Energy Agency, World Energy Outlook, 1982. Paris: Organization of Economic Cooperation and Development (OECD), 1982.

Isaak, Col. Robert, USAF, Joint Chiefs of Staff, J-5, Washington, DC. Interview, 20 October 1982.

Johnson and Packard, eds. *The Common Security Interests of Japan, the United States and NATO.* Cambridge, Massachusetts: Ballinger Publishing Company, 1981.

Kaiser, Karl, Winston Lord, Thierry de Montbrial, and David Watt. *Western Security: What has Changed? What Should be Done?* New York and

London: Council on Foreign Relations/Royal Institute of International Affairs, 1981.

Lellouche, Pierre. "Does NATO Have a Future? A European View." *The Washington Quarterly* (Summer 1982).

Moisi, Dominique. "Mitterrand's Foreign Policy: The Limits of Continuity." *Foreign Affairs* (Winter 1981/82).

Newsom, David D. "America Engulfed." *Foreign Policy*, 43 (Summer 1981).

Noyes, James H. *The Clouded Lens: Persian Gulf Security and United States Policy.* Stanford: Hoover Institute Press, 1982.

"Rapid Deployment Force: Will Europe Help America Help Europe?" *The Economist* (London) (11 December 1982).

Rapid Deployment Joint Task Force/Combat Capabilities Analysis Group. *Turkey Basing.* Background paper, 8 October 1980 (Secret).

Reed, Thomas C. "Banquet Address." *Signal* (August 1982).

Richardson, John P. "Japan: A Middle East Peace Role?" *Middle East International* (London), no. 188 (26 November, 1982).

Schwarz, Hans-Peter. "What is Wrong with U.S.-West German Relations?" *SAIS Review* (Spring 1982).

Sloan, Stanley R. "Crisis in NATO: A Problem of Leadership." *NATO Review* No. 3 (1982).

Soames, Christopher. "Why Europe and America Disagree on the Mideast." *The Washington Post* (1 December 1982).

Thompson, Scott. "The Persian Gulf and the Correlation of Forces." *International Security* 7, no. 1 (Summer 1982).

Tucker, Robert W. "The Atlantic Alliance and its Critics." *Commentary* 73 (May 1982).

US Congress, House Committee on Armed Services. *Europe and the Middle East.* Washington, DC: Government Printing Office, 23 April 1982.

US Congress, House Foreign Affairs Committee, Subcommittee on Europe and the Middle East. *NATO After Afghanistan.* Simon Lunn, Congressional Research Service, 27 October 1980.

US Congress, House Committee on Foreign Affairs. *Soviet Policy and United States Response in the Third World.* A report by the Congressional Research Service, 97th Congress, 1st Session. Washington, DC: Government Printing Office, 1981.

US Congress, Senate Committee on Foreign Relations. *NATO Today: The Alliance in Evolution.* A report, 97th Congress, 2d Session. Washington, DC: Government Printing Office, 1982.

Weinberger, Caspar W. "Additing in the Allies." *Defense.* Washington, DC: Government Printing Office, May 1982.

Willema, Herbert K., and John R. VanWingen. "Law and Power in Military Intervention: Major States after World War II." *International Studies Quarterly* 26, no. 2 (June 1982).

Windor, Philip. "Germany and the Western Alliance: Lessons from the 1980 Crises." *Adelphi Papers No. 170.* London: International Institute for Strategic Studies, 1981.

Wohlstetter. "Meeting the Threat in the Persian Gulf." *Survey* 25, no. 2 (Spring, 1980).

Yorke, Valerie. "The Gulf in the 1980's." *Chatham House Papers No. 6.* London: Royal Institute of International Affairs, 1980.

Australia, America, and Indian Ocean Security

Albinski, Henry S. *The Australian-American Security Relationship: A Regional and International Perspective.* St. Lucia, Queensland, Australia: University of Queensland Press, 1982.

Albinski, Henry S. "Australia, New Zealand and the Security of the Indian Ocean Region: Perspectives and Contributions from Outlying American Alliance Partners." Lecture, Centre for Foreign Policy Studies, Dalhousie University, Halifax, Nova Scotia, October 1982.

Albinski, Henry S. "Australia and U.S. Strategy." *Current History* (April 1982): 150–154, 186.

Albinski, Henry S. "The Importance of ANZUS." *Pacific Defence Reporter* (December 1981/January 1982): 33, 35–36, 41–42, 44–45, 47, 50–51.

Albinski, Henry S. "The Strategic Importance of the Indian Ocean: The Key Link Between East and West Asia." Lecture, National Defense University, 1983 Pacific Symposium, Washington, DC, 20–21 January 1983.

Albinski, Henry S., Director of Australian Studies and Professor of Political Science, Pennsylvania State University. Interview, 29 December 1982.

Alves, Dora. "Does ANZUS Really Matter to the U.S.?" *Pacific Defence Reporter* (July 1982): 38–39.

Anderson, Captain Robert G. (USN), Joint Chiefs of Staff, Southeast Asia Plans and Policy Branch (J–5). Interview, 17 November 1982.

Arietti, Michael R., Political Section, US Embassy, Canberra, Australia. Letter to K.J. McGuire, 2 March 1983.

Austin, Commander Michael (USN), Bureau of Political Military Affairs, Department of State. Interview, 19 November 1982.

Australian Bureau of Statistics. *Australian Yearbook 1981–1982.* Canberra: Australia Government Printing Office, 1982.

"Australasia '81: Defense." *Far Eastern Economic Review* (6 November 1981): 52–55.

Australian Parliament, Joint Committee on Foreign Affairs and Defence. *Threats to Australia's Security, Their Nature and Probability.* Canberra: Government Printing Office, 1981.

Australian Parliament, Presented by Minister for Defense D.J. Killen. "Australian Defense." Canberra: Government Printing Office, 1976.

Australian Parliament, Senate, Standing Committee on Foreign Affairs and Defense. *Australia and the Indian Ocean Region.* Canberra: Government Printing Office, 1976.

Autry, Major General Ruben (USAF). Speech delivered to a conference on Australia. Port Hedland, Northern Territory, Australia, 20 October 1982.

Ball, Desmond. *A Suitable Piece of Real Estate; American Installations in Australia.* Sydney: Hale and Iremonger, 1980.

Ball, Desmond, and J.O. Langtry. *Problems of Mobilization In Defense of Australia.* Manuka: Phoenix Defense Publications, 1980.

Ballantyne, Thomas. "Australia's Nuclear Targets." *Sydney Morning Herald* (23 November 1982): 5: 1–3.

Beakey, Dan J. *Logistics Over the Shore: Do we Need It?* National Security Affairs Monograph Series 82–6. Washington, DC: National Defense University Press, 1982.

Beazley, Kim, and Ian Clark. *The Politics of Intrusion: The Super Powers and the Indian Ocean.* Sydney: Alternative Publishing Cooperative Ltd., 1979.

Beck, Group Captain Gary (RAAF), Research Fellow, National Defense University. Frequent interviews, October 1982–March 1983.

Bell, Coral, ed. *Agenda for the Eighties: Contexts of Australian Choices in Foreign and Defence Policy.* Canberra: Australian National University Press, 1980.

Boyt, Captain George R. (USN), Action Officer, Petroleum Requirements, Chief of Naval Operations Staff, Materiel Division (OP-413D). Interview, 2 March 1983.

Bowman, Larry, and Ian Clark, eds. *The Indian Ocean in Global Politics.* Boulder, Colorado: Westview Press, 1981.

Brammill, Colin. "Australia Would Extend Laws for Islanders." *Canberra Times* (1 December 1982): 13: 1–4.

Brand, Robert, Deputy Assistant Secretary, Bureau of East Asian and Pacific Affairs, Department of State. Interviews, 26 August and 3 December 1982.

Brand, Robert, P. Hymson, and H. Indorf, eds. *Lines of Communications and Security.* National Defense University 1981 Pacific Symposium Proceedings. Washington, DC: National Defense University Press, 1981.

Brown, Gary, and Derek Woolner. *A New Aircraft Carrier for the Royal Australian Navy?* Canberra: Strategic and Defence Studies Centre, Australian National University, Working paper no. 57, 28 July 1982.

Cottrell, Alvin J., and Robert J. Hanks. *The Military Utility of the U.S. Facilities in the Philippines.* Washington, DC: The Center of Strategic and International Studies, Georgetown University, Significant Issues series, 1980.

Cranston, Frank. "Defence Interests: A Major Influence." *Canberra Times* (1 December 1982): 13: 4–5.

Davidson, Rear Admiral John (RAN). "Security and Lines of Communication in the Pacific and Indian Oceans." *Lines of Communications and Security.* Proceedings of 1981 National Defense University Pacific Symposium. Washington, DC: National Defense University Press, May 1981.

"Defending the Gulf: A Survey." *The Economist* (6 June 1981): 21–23.

"The Defence Force of Australia." *Army Quarterly and Defense Journal.* Travistock, Devon, U.K., 1977.

Djalal, Hasjim, Chairman of the Indonesian Delegation to the Law of the Sea Conference. "Economic Zones: The Concept and Its Implications." Address, National Defense University Pacific Symposium, Washington, DC, 20–21 January 1983.

Dooley, Commander William J., Chief of Naval Operations Staff, Assistant for Military Sales, Security Assistance Division (OP–63). Interview, 12 January 1983.

Dorrance, John, Country Director, Office of Australian-New Zealand Affairs, Department of State. Frequent interviews, August 1982–March 1983.

Ellison, John H. "Hands (Defense Industrial) Across the Pacific." *Pacific Defence Reporter* (November 1982): 12–14, 16–17.

Fabrie, Robert. "SLOC Security." Lecture, National Defense University Pacific Symposium, Washington, DC, 20–21 January 1983.

Finney, John, Bureau of Political Military Affairs, Department of State. Interview, 26 October 1982.

Foreign Economic Trends: Australia. Canberra: American Embassy, November 1982.

"Future of the Cocos." *The Canberra Times* (2 December 1982): 5: 1–3.

Gelber, Harry G. "Australian Strategic Perspectives." Lecture, The National Defense University 1980 Trans-Pacific Security Issues Symposium, Washington, DC, 28–29 May 1980.

Gelber, Harry G. "Australia, The Pacific and the United States in the 1980's." *Comparative Strategy.* New York: Strategic Studies Center, SRI International, Crane, Russack & Co. Inc., 1981.

Gelber, Harry G. "Australia, the United States and the Strategic Balance." *Australian Outlook* (August 1982): 12–21.

Gelber, Harry G., Chairman of the Department of Political Science, University of Tasmania. Interview, 9 November 1982.

"General Information Notes on H.M.A.S. Stirling." Royal Australian Navy, undated.

Gilmour, Trevor. "Bombers Stretch Their Wings." *West Australian* (23 November 1982).

Goldenstein, Captain G.R. (USN), Chief of Naval Operations Staff, Head, Carrier Warfare Branch, Carrier and Air Station Programs Division (OP–551). Interview, 17 November 1982.

Goldrich, Sub Lieutenant J.V.P. (RAN) and Sub Lieutenant P.D. Jones (RAN). "The Royal Australian Navy—A Progress Report." *U.S. Naval Institute Proceedings* (July 1981): 112–115.

Grazebrook, A.W. "Putting A Price on *Invincible.*" *Pacific Defence Reporter* (November 1981): 21–23.

Grazebrook, A.W. "After *Invincible*—Where Next?," *Pacific Defence Reporter* (September 1982) 25, 27–28, 30, 32–33.

Grazebrook, A.W. "Australia's Maritime Air Power—Where Next?" *Pacific Defence Reporter* (July 1982): 8–12.

Griffiths, David R. "Australia Seeks Aerospace Self-Reliance." *Aviation Week and Space Technology* (17 March 1980): 44–45.

"Handbook for Ships: HMAS Stirling." Royal Australian Navy, December 1981.

Hanks, Robert J. *The Cape Route: Imperiled Western Lifeline.* Cambridge, Massachusetts: Institute for Foreign Policy Analysis, 1981.

Hartnett, Sir Laurence. "Make Our Munitions or Perish." Letter to the Editor, *Pacific Defence Reporter* (June 1981): 58.

Hill-Norton, Admiral of the Fleet, Lord Peter. "Australia's Place in Western Defense Strategy." Lecture, Joint Seminar of the British-Australian Society and Royal United Services Institute, London, 8 October 1980.

"The Hornet Keeps Its Sting," *Pacific Defence Reporter* (November 1981): 59.

The International Institute for Strategic Studies (London). "The Military Balance 1982/83." *Air Force Magazine* (December 1982): 61–70, 73–76.

J.J. Henry Co., Inc. *Essex Class Refurbishment.* Report no. 2033–00. 26 October 1981.

Kelly, Paul. "Bowen Writes Reagan on N-Ban." *Sydney Morning Herald* (6 November 1982): 10: 1–2.

Killen, D.J. "The Philosophy of Australian Defence." *Pacific Defence Reporter* (June 1981): 4–6.

Langtry, J.O., and Desmond Ball. "Australia's Strategic Situation and Its Implications for Australian Industry." *Pacific Defence Reporter* (February 1981): 36–42.

Langtry, J.O., Robert O'Neill, and Jolika Tie. *Australia's Defence Resources.* Canberra: Australian National University, 1978.

The Library of Congress, Congressional Research Service, Foreign Affairs and National Defense Division. *Rapid Deployment Joint Task Force Recast as a Unified Command.* 10 December 1982.

Marfiak, Commander Thomas (USN), and Commander Morris Kemple (USN), Chief of Naval Operations Staff, Strategic Concepts Study Group, Strategy, Plans and Policy Division (OP–60). Interview, 9 November 1982.

Major, Captain James (USN), Commander-in-Chief, US Pacific Fleet (CINCPAC) Staff. Interview, 10 February 1983.

McCarthy, John. "Problems in Australian Foreign Policy." *The Australian Journal of Politics and History* (December 1977): 331.

McKinnon, M. "McVeigh Spells Out Cocos Islands Options." *The Australian* (30 November, 1982): 3: 3–4.

"Memorandum of Understanding on Logistic Support Between the Government of Australia and the Government of United States of America," 18 March 1980.

Moore, Captain John E. (RN, FRGS), ed. *Jane's Fighting Ships.* London: Poulton House, 1982.

"New Carrier Not Worth It, Defence Group Claims." *Sydney Morning Herald* (27 August 1982): 2: 1–4.

O'Neill, Robert, and D.M. Horner, eds. *Australian Defence Policy for the 1980s.* St. Lucia, Australia: University of Queensland Press, 1982.

O'Neill, Robert, ed. *The Defence of Australia: Fundamental New Aspects.* Canberra: The Australian National University Press, 1977.

O'Neill, Robert. "Diplomacy and Defence." In Bell (ed), *Agenda for the Eighties.* Canberra: The Australian National University Press, 1980. 45–64.

O'Neill, Robert, Director, International Institute for Strategic Studies, London. Interview, 17 November 1982.

O'Sullivan, Paul, First Secretary, Australian Embassy, Washington, DC. Interview, 31 March, 1983.

Overseas Trade of Australia: Comparative and Summary Tables II. Canberra: Australian Bureau of Statistics, 1982.

Pacific Defence Reporter (Annual Reference edition). Melbourne: Peter Isaacson Publications Ltd., 1982.

"Phase-out of Bases Predicted." *Washington Times* (7 September 1982): 6: 1–2.

Pinwill, William. "Sinclair Eases Entry for N-Ships." *Australian* (12 September 1982).

Pritchett, W.B. "Defending Australia and Its Interests." *Pacific Defence Reporter* (July 1982): 58–60, 62.

"Proteus: The Case for Sea-borne Air Power." *Pacific Defence Reporter* (October 1979): 8.

Radic, Leonard. "Most Favor Visits by U.S. Nuclear Ships." *Melbourne Age* (25 October 1982): 9.

Richardson, Michael. "The RAAF's Role in South-East Asia." *Pacific Defence Reporter* (October 1982): 47–48, 50.

Rusbridge, Wing Commander P.J. (RAAF). "A Military View on the Future of the Australian Aircraft Industry." *Defence Force Journal*, no. 28 (May-June 1981): 5–12.

Sinclair, Ian. Untitled address to the Australian Defence Association. *Commonwealth Record* (November 1982): 1648–1651.

Snow, Deborah. "New Northern Territory Base Likely for the RAAF." *Australian Financial Review* (26 November 1982): 22.

Snow, Deborah. "U.S. Softens Its Attitude toward ALP." *Australian Financial Review* (8 November 1982): 16–18.

Snow, Commodore John P. (RAN), Naval Attache, Australian Embassy, Washington, DC. Interview, 20 October 1982.

Snow, Commodore John P. (RAN). Telephone conversation, 8 March 1983.

Sowell, Lewis C., Jr. *Base Development and Rapid Deployment Force: A Window to the Future.* National Security Affairs Monograph series 82–5. Washington, DC: National Defense University Press, 1982.

Tahtinen, Dale R. *Arms In the Indian Ocean: Interests and Challenges.* Washington, DC: American Enterprise Institute, 1977.

Tow, William J. "ANZUS and American Security." *Survival* (November-December 1981): 261–270.

Tow, William J. "Asia-Pacific Alliance Systems and Transregional Linkages." *Naval War College Review* (September-October 1981): 32–54.

The US Congress, House Committee on Foreign Affairs. *U.S. Security Interests in the Persian Gulf.* Staff study. Washington, DC: US Government Printing Office, 1981.

The US Congress, Senate Committee on Foreign Relations. *Prospects on NATO's Southern Flank.* Delegation report. Washington, DC: US Government Printing Office, 1980.

Viner, Ian. "Building Up the Defense Industries." *Pacific Defence Reporter* (September, 1982): 9–10, 12–13.

Wall, Patrick, ed. *The Indian Ocean and the Threat to the West.* London: Stacey International, 1975.

Wettern, Desmond. "Will Britain Let *Invincible* Go?" *Pacific Defence Reporter* (June 1982): 20–21.

Willis, Vice Admiral Sir James (RAN). "Why We Bought *Invincible*." *Pacific Defence Reporter* (April 1982): 61–62, 64, 73.

Young, Thomas Durell. *ANZUS in the Indian Ocean: Strategic Considerations.* Geneva: Institut Universitaire des Hautes Études Internationales, 1982.

Zakheim, Dov. S. "Toward a Western Approach to the Indian Ocean." *Survival* (January/February 1980): pp. 14–17.

☆ U.S. GOVERNMENT PRINTING OFFICE: 1984-421-686:10001